D0734398

Dr. Science's
Book of
Shocking
Domestic Revelations

Also by Dr. Science (with Rodney)

The Official Dr. Science Big Book of Science

BOOK OF

SHOCKING

DOMESTIC

REVELATIONS

with DAN COFFEY
and MERLE KESSLER

by

DR. SCIENCE

WILLIAM MORROW AND COMPANY, INC.

NEW YORK

All interior photographs courtesy of the San Francisco History Room, San Francisco Public Library.

It is the policy of William Morrow and Company, Inc., and its imprints and affiliates, recognizing the importance of preserving what has been written, to print the books we publish on acid-free paper, and we exert our best efforts to that end.

LIBRARY OF CONGRESS CATALOGING-IN-PUBLICATION DATA

Dr. Science.
Dr. Science's book of shocking domestic revelations / Dr. Science (Dan Coffey), Merle Kessler.
p. cm.
ISBN 0-688-11444-X
1. Science—Humor. 2. American wit and humor. I. Shoales, Ian, 1949– II. Title. III. Title: Book of shocking domestic revelations.
PN6231.S4D6 1993
818′.5402—dc20 93-16375
CIP

Printed in the United States of America

First Edition

1 2 3 4 5 6 7 8 9 10

BOOK DESIGN BY PATRICE FODERO

CONTENTS

	Introduction: An Urgent Message to America	9
1	Getting Started	19
2	Paying Through the Nose	35
3	Employment Woes	55
4	Your Home and You	81
5	Intimate Details	119
6	Education and Home Entertainment	151
7	The Future	169
	The Final Chapter: Your Dream House	185
	Appendix	195
	Glossary	203

Dr. Science's Book of Shocking Domestic Revelations

INTRODUCTION: AN URGENT MESSAGE TO AMERICA

KNOWLEDGE AT THE CROSSROADS

Forty years ago, the key of curiosity was all you needed to open the treasure chest of Scientific data. Everything was common knowledge. The table of elements, the theory of relativity, the Phrygian codes of Mithras—all were part of a corpus of information which lay at the feet of everyone, from foxy Grandpa to slow Uncle Bob. You could have stopped any schoolboy on the street, asked him the speed of light, and you wouldn't have been arrested! Today's kids, *even those with a fifth grade education*, don't know Planck's Constant from the Heisenberg Uncertainty Principle. What went wrong?

A lot of things.

A SIMPLE DIAGRAM

All human knowledge until 1950 can be expressed by the following Square of Opposition:

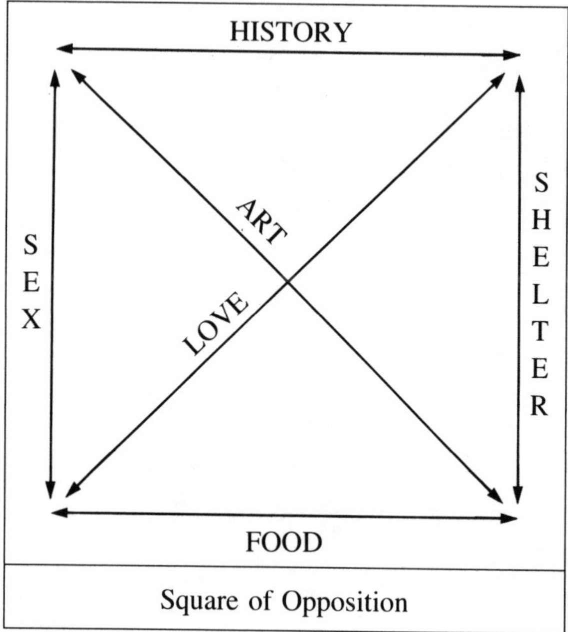

Square of Opposition

It was elegant, clear, and direct.

This tidy box not only held *everything*, it boasted efficient methods for neatly folding information into it. Alas, the habits of untold centuries have been kicked. We no longer have this box. One might say that Pandora's box has been opened, unleashing chaos. And the study of chaos, ironically, has become the only Science that matters.

WHOM DO WE BLAME?

EDUCATION

In the sixties, teachers began to whine, "Number crunching is too boring," and, "Who cares about the speed of light? I'm never going to go that fast anyway." They began to spend valuable class time not on memorization of random numbers but frog dissection, which (fascinating though it is) just did not fill pliant brains with the hard facts needed to populate undersea colonies, increase sorghum production, or intimidate those less powerful than ourselves.

And while our teachers busily color-coded student files, the Russians slogged ahead of us. If the Soviet system hadn't collapsed (an event I predicted back in 1956*), we would have been up the creek without a paddle. As it is, we are up the creek, but at least we still have a paddle. My paddle. You're holding it in your hands.

It's this book.

POLITICS

Ask citizens today to visualize a politician, and some will see a grinning glad-hander with one hand in your cookie jar; some a sinister figure with slicked-back hair who raises money quasi-legally to support minor revolutions in parts of the globe you've never heard of.

To others, politicians are selfless creatures, distant kin to the faeries of Celtic lore, gifted with the ability to flit from business to business, bestowing blessings with the tip of a magic wand. To the fawning lobbyist the inner being of a politician is luminous. In the presence of certain special-interest groups, some senators even glow in the dark.

I myself have worn through dozens of soles trudging up The Hill trying to persuade Congress to ease restrictions on noxious odors. (As my own research has proven, big stinks are essential to Science.) I have urged my two-color brochure on many congressional aides. I have been politely shown many doors. I have shouted myself hoarse under many a senator's bedroom window. All to no avail.

But others followed in my footsteps, well-scrubbed men and women from major corporations, bearing shiny briefcases full of money! (P.S. They got the job done!)

***Communism Will Fail in '91!*. Laundromat Publishing, Retroactive Copyright 1956.

In America, anything worth doing can only be done by those whose lives won't change much if it's done or not. And yet, they're the only ones with money. Faced with this paradox, special interests shrug and say to themselves cheerfully, "Spend it or lose it!" We swing wildly between political desires—for Big Government or anarchy, laissez-faire capitalism or federal industrial policy, prayer in schools or multicultural homework. This leads inevitably to confusion, ambivalence, low voter turnout, and an unhealthy obsession with professional sports.

So long as we persist in viewing our all-too-human representatives as angels or devils, one's five-billion-dollar boondoggle may indeed be another's linear accelerator, this citizen's pork barrel will be that one's Pork Institute, and my National Museum of Toxic Fumes, for which I've spent half a lifetime seeking funds, will remain a dream.

Don't you think the time has come to break these bonds and be free?

So does this Scientist.

CODEPENDENCY

So what *did* happen to our can-do pioneer spirit?

Mom and Dad used to spend long hours of quality time with their offspring, guiding them through tricky quadratic equations over tasty batches of yeast-sprinkled popcorn and buttermilk. But Mom and Dad also made sure the so-called traditional family values stopped at the front door. They were savvy enough to boot their children out of the house at the onset of puberty, thus instilling in their youngsters the terror necessary to face life head on.

Not so today. Today's kids stay at home well into their thirties, taking illegal drugs, besotting themselves with malt liquor, disrespecting their elders, and stealing rare coins from Dad's collection to play the lottery. Many of them are television producers.

WHAT CAN BE DONE?

Voting, education, and participation in even a dysfunctional family unit all require one thing: permanent residency. Yet this societal demand to stay in one place is directly at odds with the demands of the id! The so-called Mick Jagger of the psyche doesn't want to be tied down; no, the Midnight Rambler of the soul would stay up all night every night if we let it, hitching around the country and getting its head together, eating only when it's hungry and sleeping only when it falls over.

I call this American dichotomy the Roy/Dale Syndrome. Half of the self is Roy, who wants to ride the range on a powerful steed, singing the cattle to sleep. The other half is Dale, who wants the Sons of the Pioneers out of the bunkhouse *pronto* to make room for all the orphans she plans to adopt.

Clearly, America is in a crisis. And we cannot reconcile the estranged Roy and Dale of the spirit because we are plagued by

1. too much undigested information, and
2. ignorance of the real information needed to survive into the twenty-first century.

In response to the crisis, I began to conceive new ways of managing raw data. The concept of a book, though alarmingly analog, seemed like the perfect vehicle.

TOWARD A SOLUTION

Not so long ago, having given up on public funding for my museum, I was trying to raise funds privately. Toward that end, I was going door to door, selling my own line of chemistry sets for toddlers, KinderKem™. (If we wish to lead the world down the path of Science, we must begin with our own young.) This easily portable

kit (still available by the way) contains sturdy glassware, a mini Bunsen burner, and every chemical a bright three-year-old would need to create life in the bathtub.

I was explaining the benefits of KinderKem™ to an overly suspicious young father, patiently telling him that any slight burning sensation his child might experience would only be a side effect of the heavily diluted acid included with the kit at no extra charge. It is totally harmless! Symptoms can be relieved immediately by washing the affected area in cold water! He was not convinced. The next thing I knew I was nursing a black eye and mild concussion in my reasonably priced hotel room in Oklahoma City.

I can't say I was depressed by what had happened, exactly. I am not capable of mood swings. My passions (and my need for sleep) are regulated with daily vitamin injections. But I was feeling as close to pensive as it is possible for me to get. Then I did something I hadn't done since 1958: I turned on the television.

What I saw on that television that late sultry summer afternoon changed my life. It was the story, apparently, of a man named Brady. I can no longer recall specific details of the program, beyond the fact that it was fairly amusing, especially when this Brady fellow installed a pay telephone in the home to reinforce some value or another among various family members. Needless to say, the kids learned their lesson, the exact nature of which escapes me.* Be that as it may, as I lay there on the lumpy mattress, absorbing the gestalt of the audio-visual experience, three factors immediately jarred my consciousness:

(1) The program began by displaying a mysterious grid, with nine squares each containing a face from the extended Brady clan, smiling one upon the other. The open warmth of those happy faces! The mathematical rigor of the grid! It made me almost weep with joy!

(2) The actor playing Mr. Brady was a fellow named Robert Reed. I have entertained a theory for years that a society of men named Bob secretly rule the world. (True, we have had no presidents named Bob, but they frequently surround themselves with Bobs—McNamara, Kennedy, Mosbacher, etc.) Here was more evidence to be filed away in the vast database of my mind.

(3) The actress playing the Brady maid, Alice, was Ann B. Davis, whom I immediately recognized from the program I'd seen the last time I watched television, the excellent *Love That Bob* (Bob again!), starring Robert (!) Cummings. She played a character named Schultzy. *The same actress!* Surely this was more than mere coincidence.

*The so-called traditional family values, unfortunately, are foreign to my nature, perhaps because my childhood was spent in a controlled laboratory situation, after which my father, Miloscz Szcienscz (who studied with the immortal Tesla), over the objections of my sentimental mother, Rudolfa, the famed *chanteuse*, set me adrift in a hot-air balloon, in which I drifted, carefree, over three continents until I attained my majority.

Suddenly I found myself overcome by the combination of the day's events. Some would say I passed out. I prefer to think I entered a trance state. As proof, when I awoke some three hours later, I found myself lying on my back in the middle of the carpet. Several leaves of the hotel stationery thoughtfully provided by the management lay on my chest, neatly pinned to my shirt. As I removed them, I noticed they were covered with my distinctive bold handwriting. These of course were the now-legendary Oklahoma Auguries. (See Appendix for the text in full.)

This "automatic writing" provoked disturbing questions. How had photographer Bob Cummings, bachelor swinger of the fifties, evolved into architect Bob Reed, loving father of six? Why had the gadabout playboy turned in the wings of his private jet to grapple with crabgrass in suburbia? Why had all those ambitious supermodels stopped doing the Peppermint Twist with half-baked Hefners to join supermom Florence Henderson as helpmates to hubbies in tract housing? And Ann B. Davis—why didn't she age?

Thanks to the grid of smiling faces filtered through my pain and mild delirium, I slowly began to grope my way toward some answers. I suddenly saw a way to bring the traditional Square of Opposition into line with the latter half of the twentieth century.

Excited, my hands trembling, I began to scrawl on the hotel stationery. After a mere four hours, I came up with this:

Bob "Bob" Cummings	large urban dwelling	Ann B. Davis
supermodels	ranch-style home	*supermom* Florence Henderson
Ann B. Davis	apartment or flat	Bob "Dad" Reed

Good, yes, but what did it mean?

I wasn't content with this breakthrough. I'm no television actor, content to rest on my residuals, waiting anxiously for phone calls. I'm a Scientist. I kept the television on all night. Through a haze of *Remington Steele* and *MacGyver* encore presentations, I wore the hotel-provided pencils to nubs and used up both sides of the remaining ten sheets of paper included in the price of my room.

It was worth it. It became the outline for this book.

PARADIGM REGAINED!

Obviously, we are all in terrible danger. I believe that our homes are trying to kill us. And yet, is the outside world not trying to kill us as well? How do we weigh the two dangers? How do we stay in the house long enough to avoid the dangers of the outside world, like "Bob" Reed, yet venture in the world long enough to protect ourselves from the dangers of the home, like "Bob" Cummings?

This book, guided by *The Brady Bunch*, the Two Bobs Theory, and the Roy/Dale Syndrome, is here to help. Not unlike a window, this elegant nonfiction work will allow us to look out upon the world through beautiful latticework, superimposed on it at random! The world can also gaze upon *us*. Naturally, on the world's side of this book the pattern will be reversed and the words all backward, but this is as close to the hippie ideal of communal sharing as we can expect from the wretched thing we call modern existence.

Here then is the modest aim of this volume: to explain the dangers of the world to you, gentle reader, in terms even an idiot can understand. Everything from soup to nuts to bolts. All you have to do is admit your ignorance, and this book will do the rest.

TO DO AND SEE

1. How effective would Pierce Brosnan have been in the role of James Bond had he not been tied up with *Remington Steele*?
2. MacGyver can make a high explosive out of chewing gum, a woman's barrette, and wallpaper. What can you do?
3. What are the Phrygian codes of Mithras?
4. What is it about reasonably priced hotel rooms in Oklahoma City that leads one to morbid introspection?
5. If you were to check in to a reasonably priced hotel room in your immediate area, turn on the television, and try to think, what with hearing retired railroad employees hacking all night through the thin walls, do you think you could come up with a model or grid of some kind on which all of human knowledge could be superimposed? I doubt it.
6. (True or False) Unprocessed data can cause actual physical harm.
7. Is Alex Trebek a Scientist or a savant?
8. Is Mick Jagger a Roy or a Dale?
9. Using the Two Bobs Theory, which Bob would Mick Jagger be? Charlie Watts?
10. Would you be willing to write your congressman in support of a National Museum of Toxic Fumes?

1

GETTING STARTED

BACK TO THE BASICS

Every journey begins with a single step. Omelet composition requires massive egg destruction. Before we sit by the window to watch the world go by, we must first have walls—otherwise we are lugging around huge panes of glass to no purpose. Yet to build even the most modest of homes usually involves the bribery of housing officials.

And so it is with the book you hold in your hands. I am asking you not only to begin your journey of self-improvement with the fabled single step, I am asking you to make that step in my shoes. At the end of our journey there's a cozy cottage and all the eggs you can eat. Trust me. And you can keep the shoes, my friends. I have more.

THE FOUNDATION OF MATTER

We used to believe, foolishly, that atoms were the furniture in the living rooms we call molecules. We now know that atoms themselves are tiny living rooms, crammed with the knickknacks we call subatomic particles, and that molecules are vast housing complexes in the decaying urban environment we call the material world.

Like the popular singer Madonna, we are indeed living in that material world. True, most of us don't live as well as she does, but then most of us don't have her pep, either. Despite everything, it's still pep, or energy, that runs things around here.

THE NEW PHYSICS

From fast-food cheeseburgers to the latest cheap plastic toy that disintegrates as soon as you get it home, today's goods only last as long as the gaudy trappings that house them. So it is with the basic units of life: They are mere justifications for packaging. This is called the New Physics and need not concern us here except to demonstrate that all matter as we know it consists of boxes within boxes.

For most of this book, we will be rummaging through the middle series of these boxes, located roughly at the halfway point between the lowly quark and the infinite majesty of the universe:

- *Your Body*
- *Your House*
- *The World Around You.*

Your Body is more than just a leaky sac of chromosomes, it's your home. Home to whatever you choose to call your soul, and home to your brain, which in turn is home to your thoughts. Just as the skull encloses the cauliflower-like organ of the brain, so *Your House* encloses you and protects you from *The World Around You*, which in turn (thanks to our protective envelope of atmosphere and gravity) keeps us from flying off into the vacuum of space and imploding.

YOUR BODY

Though it is the least important element in the miniseries of physical objects posited above, the body requires our best attention. Like the car, which we use only to get us from place of abode to place of work or vacation and back, the body is taken for granted until something goes wrong with it.

Food, exercise, moderate sexual activity, wholesome hobbies, and backbreaking labor at substandard wages—such, traditionally, have been the fuels that energize the body. As we will see, many of these traditions have become outmoded and deserve to be confined to the dustbin of history.

The important thing to remember is: The body is a basket for the brain, with limbs, nothing more, nothing less. We were all wild nomads once, torching the flimsy tents of our rivals with fierce grins on our lips. Those days are gone. Today, we'd probably all be happier if we were a handful of gray matter floating in a sterilized glass bowl filled with liquid nutrients. But we're not, and so must act accordingly.

YOUR HOUSE

As polarized lenses protect the naked eye from harmful ultraviolet rays, so the home protects the fleshy shell enveloping the seat of our being, the brain. It is the first line of defense against the world. Nothing is more important than the home. This is why so many apartment dwellers appear nervous and ill at ease, and why so few street people are physicists.

I have eliminated the need for permanent housing in my life, but the ascetic life-style I have chosen is not for everybody. Not many people can go through life lacking a base of security. One of the services this book hopes to render is to identify those qualities that make up what we call The Home, and provide the means to effect useful substitutes. It's a wicked world out there. Everybody needs some defense.

THE WORLD AROUND YOU

From vicious stinging insects to the insensitive bullies who sign our paychecks, the world outside our doors seems expressly designed to throw monkey wrenches into the machinery of our inner peace. This is no illusion. The world is out to get you.

This is exactly why The Home is so important. What is The Home? Its basics are simplicity itself: walls, roof, and electricity, in the middle of which we stand like Mom and Dad Brady, smiling our brave smiles, as secure in our delusions as a king and queen on the eve of revolution, waving from the parapets as the surly mob closes in.

WHERE DO YOU LIVE?

There is a comparison I often use to make a point with the occasional bright-faced youngster who calls me mentor—the comparison of the human to the turtle. As the human has the house, has not the turtle its shell—to protect, warm, and comfort? As the human has a job, has not the turtle its quest for tiny finned creatures to devour? And, as we humans seek pleasure in diversion, does not the turtle bask motionless in a tiny patch of sunlight?

Judging by the looks of comprehension which dawn on the faces of my sporadic pupils, this comparison hits home. "I am turtlelike in many important ways," think these troubled adolescents. Fair enough. But what about the rest of it? The factors that separate us from cold-blooded reptiles? What about neckties? Eyeliner? Warm young?

Read on.

Say the word *home* to a group of a hundred people, and different images will be conjured among them. A certain percentage—five, let's say—will visualize a little scrubbed fenced-in cottage by the sea. Another ten will picture a sturdy brick house on an elm-lined street. Still another ten will think of payment schedules and leaky roofs. Others will see the dank apartment, in which they dwell in solitude. Some will think, "wasn't built in a day," having thought you'd asked them to free-associate to the word *Rome*. (Caution: When leading group visualizations, speak slowly and clearly.) Some will not see anything at all, because they weren't paying attention.

The point is this: Get a hundred people in a room and you can pretty much get them to visualize anything. But if you approach these same hundred people individually and ask them to free-associate to words you've written carefully on your clipboard, you'll get a hundred doors slammed in your face. Why?

The answer lies in the difference between a multipurpose room and a private dwelling. The former is a windowless room full of folding chairs, illuminated by harsh fluorescent light. The latter is a different kettle of fish altogether. Let's bring our clipboard and sketchpad to Main Street, Anywhere, USA (much like Disneyworld, only slightly larger), to examine that phenomenon which politicians call housing.

THE ROOF

Perhaps you have children. If you do, I don't doubt that you have spent many hours lurching across the floor on all fours, a blanket covering your body, as mobs of preschoolers leaped on your back screaming, "Turtle, turtle!"

This primitive ritual brings us back to the useful turtle metaphor I used in the previous section, and points out the limitations of the metaphor. No self-respecting turtle would allow toddlers to pound its back with tiny little fists. And no self-respecting human would sit placidly on a mossy log in the middle of a dirty lake. Not for hours anyway. We don't have the patience.

Yet, oddly, we do have the patience to pummel a roof with hammers, like small children playing turtle with a large immovable object. Roof repair is one of the many atavisms to which humans so often revert.

Take a look at roof repair. What do you see?

You see a man, perhaps hired to do the job, busily shingling or sliding slate into place, jigsawing geometric patterns out of verge-board, hammering the curve into a stately mansard. He is singing or cursing, depending on how the chore is coming. From time to time the air is filled with human speech: "Yo, hand me up that two by four, Bo!"; "Here she comes!"; "How's it goin' up there, Joe?"; "Put your back into it, boys!" Who can resist a swell of pride and pleasure at the sights and sounds of rough workmen overcharging at their labor?

And yet there's more going on here. The hammering on the roof is a tacky reminder of the drumming our primitive ancestors once performed by the fire. The hammer is also the club once used to fight enemies or KO an evening meal. It was the first tool, an early weapon, and the reason why we have hardware stores and Tim Allen today.

Moreover, here we are in the twentieth century, still fighting the ancient enemies of weather, darkness, that urge to ramble, and neighbors. Without that roof over the head, after all, a house is just four walls and soggy linoleum.

Beyond the purely physical protection from the elements, the roof offers us psychological protection as well. As we lie rigidly on our backs at night, trying frantically to fall asleep, the roof is all that separates us from that unspeakable void, sprinkled with stars and shrill birds, from which all humans shrink.

So what is it that prevents us from carrying a waterproof insulated shell—not unlike an umbrella—and setting up home wherever we find ourselves at the end of the day?

Many things. Our spouses, for one. I tried this once and my ex-wife—Elaine, I believe it was—was out of the hogan and into divorce court like a shot. Then there's the desire for permanence. We all used to follow the buffalo herds for a living, but today the life of a nomad, outside of the collective unconscious, is pretty much confined to surfers, beatniks, and visiting professors. Try to find a buffalo these days, much less dog its heels bareback on a pinto and sling arrows at it! Our income level also determines whether we live in a box in the park or a penthouse overlooking the park. Not too many top executives are in the habit of Dumpster diving. More's the pity. Just last week I found a set of stereo speakers as tall as I am! Even as I write this, the windows are vibrating as I listen to Wagner in the privacy of my research sanctum, the knobs turned as far right as they will go. Let the neighbors complain! This is music! This is life!

You can't do that in the park either. But I'm getting ahead of myself.

Obviously, the main reason human beings seek permanent shelter is the desire for electricity. And if you're going to have electricity, you've got to have walls.

THE WALLS

More than a blank space on which to hang wallpaper, our walls are our prison, our protection from the winds, the solid space between windows, and a shield from prying eyes. They house and disguise the mysterious force we call electricity, the blood of the modern world.

And walls are a cost-effective way to keep a roof suspended in mid-air. Without them, we would be forced to rely on anti-gravitational force fields to keep a ceiling above us, force fields that are at once costly, harmful to the environment, and violate all physical laws as we know them.

A Brief History of Walls

The wall today takes its historical cue from the Great Wall of China. Why a Great Wall? To honor the emperor, to give slave labor something to do, to provide protection from ruthless invaders, to restrict immigration, to make a space available for posters and graffiti, and to fill out the alarmingly brief list of wonders of the world. We have, alas, but seven others (see Appendix).

But even the fabled wealth of Cathay could not finish the job. Only one wall was completed. And the Great Roof of China, which Marco Polo and Christopher Columbus both gave their lives in a vain attempt to find, remains little more than a fabulous rumor, lost in the mists of time.

From the Great Wall's prototype, it was a short jump to Babylon, the Tower of Babel, the Great Library of Alexandria, the Wall of Jericho, and hence the Parthenon, the Acropolis, cruel Roman arenas, cathedrals, snug Dutch cottages, and so on, down to the half-empty office buildings and substandard housing we enjoy today.

HOME WIRING

Unlike the turtle, your house is a nervous critter. Inside its walls, just under the mildewed plaster and lath, run miles and miles of copper wire that make up your home's nervous system.

Like everything else, these wires get tired and frayed. Eventually, they snap. Then your house becomes what psychiatrists call "neurotic."

Even though most psychiatrists are themselves neurotic, their mental problems don't guarantee that juice will flow the next time you flip the switch. So instead of blaming the medical community, you'll have to gain some savvy about wiring. Either that or hire a professional.

This book strongly suggests that you save your money and do it yourself. Dr. Science has made a career out of ignoring the so-called experts. In doing so he has become the expert of experts, *Expertissimus Rex* they may have called him in ancient Rome, if they had known Latin as well as Dr. Science does.

The History of Home Wiring

The Romans had a crude form of wiring, using lime juice to transport raw electrons from *duracella*, plaster pots filled with potash and cinnabar. Dried snakes, soaked in lime juice and laid head to tail, carried the current from each *duracellum* to a jerking frog leg.

Historians disagree about what the Romans had in mind. Were they only interested in making frog legs jump, or did they put electricity to other uses? Sadly, only a few lava-encrusted samples from Pompeii exist to help us put the puzzle together.

We do know that the Romans loved putting puzzles together, to form what they called mosaics. Perhaps electricity powered some proto–light bulb that allowed puzzle-piecing to continue after dark. We are certain that whatever knowledge the Romans possessed about electricity died with the fall of the Roman Empire, not to surface again until 1743 in the laboratory of the Belgian Frederic Rayovac.

Rayovac was a harpsichord tuner by trade, and an amateur Scientist by avocation. He was attempting to create the world's first electronic synthesizer, a machine so large it had to be installed in the walls of his home.

The synthesizer used electricity to excite frog legs into banging against drums, bells, and overexcited rats, whose yelps approximated the modern-day "sample and hold" synthesizer patch.

Rayovac's synthesizer, alas, was a commercial, artistic, and domestic failure. Its costly construction brought about his financial ruin, the noises it made were judged by the musicians of the day to be "horrible and demonic," and his wife divorced him, taking the kids and what was left of his bank accounts.

Frederic Rayovac died, penniless and insane, in a tuberculosis sanitarium near what is today a Brussels discotheque. But the wiring he installed for his ill-fated synthesizer has become, ironically, the industry standard for homes and small businesses.

Some Common Home Wiring Problems and What to Do About Them

First, remove the fuse or turn the circuit breaker to Off. This is modern man's way of appeasing the gods of electricity. Once this step is taken, you will not be as prone to random electrocution. Having been appeased, the gods will only electrocute you on purpose.

Secondly you must ascertain the nature of the problem. Will nothing work, or only those appliances whose names begin with the letter *M*? Electricity is a capricious and clever force, one that delights in playing both friend and foe.

There is no logic behind an outage. Electrons are rarely logical. Their mercurial personalities don't take the time for orderly thought. They act quickly, impulsively, zipping at nearly light speed from one task to another.

Remember Reddy Kilowatt, the first electron to be photographed? He was also the first nonhuman to become a member of the American Federation of Television and Radio Artists, beating out Lassie by a mere three weeks. (Contrary to popular belief, Rin Tin Tin was *not* a member of AFTRA. Rinty was, however, president of the Screen Actors Guild for many years, ousted only when he refused to "speak" before the House Un-American Activities Committee. Rinty died, embittered and penniless, in 1954.)

Reddy worked day and night for almost thirty years, and still bungled his finances so badly he was hounded by creditors for most of his life. When he died, the IRS confiscated his collection of filaments and toaster coils. So you see, logical thought and careful, well-planned actions are not the way of electricity.

But getting back to you. There you are, in your basement, standing in a pool of water in front of the fuse box. You know something's wrong, but you haven't the faintest idea where to begin to fix it. To find out why, we must go back to your childhood.

Wasn't there a day when you were chastised by a parent for sticking a bread knife into an electrical outlet? Sure, the voltage hurt, but wasn't that parental scolding more long-lasting? Could this be why, some thirty-odd years later, you have an icky feeling when it comes to electricity? Why you can see that there's something wrong with the picture yet you don't know what it is? Why your father didn't teach you the manly arts of home repair? Why your mother was so withdrawn, so disappointed by life?

And what about the time you stuck a penny in a fuse box because there was no spare fuse, and you were too busy to go to the store and get one? Did anyone ever replace it with a real fuse? Has the building burned down by now? Are you responsible for the deaths of innocent children?

Those sad faces come to you, floating just before your face.

"*J'accuse!*" they shout, in French, for no discernible reason. You try to speak, but only the dull hum of a fluorescent light fixture comes from your open mouth.

Time was when it got dark out, on a clear night you could see the stars. Now you have to drive twenty miles away from civilization to approximate what the seeing must have been like in long ago pre-electric days. And at home it often occurs to you that yes, people *do* look better in candlelight. It occurs to you that this wonderful electric force may not be such a good friend after all.

So step out of the puddle, go upstairs, and turn off the basement light. Enough is enough. In its own time, all the wiring in your house will fail. Then you will feel a serenity man has not known since Frederic Rayovac tortured his first frog.

FYI...

It's true that we lose more heat in a house by building a fire in a fireplace than we gain, but this only means you should build fires in the summer. It's an extremely efficient means of cooling a home.

Never turn the switch on a three-way light bulb backward.

Experiments like this should only be performed in the presence of a trained Scientist, using robot manipulation with the operator safely shielded behind three feet of solid lead. If you were to turn the switch backward, the light would get dimmer and dimmer, much as you'd expect. But then something really scary would happen. After the third setting, instead of going off, the light will begin to suck all ambient energy into itself, sending this energy back to the power company to be recycled and sent to us at the regular rates.

The power companies are very much in favor of home experiments along this line. In fact, the fliers they enclose with your power bill, the ones nobody reads, constantly suggest trying this experiment. Every once in a while, some lonely shut-in reads one of these fliers and turns the switch backward. The paramedics who clean up such a scene say it's not a pretty sight.

Batteries may run on D cell, C, AA, and AAA, but none runs on simple A or B. If anyone should try to sell you a flashlight that runs on those batteries, tell him, "Thanks, but no thanks!" The fact is that anyone peddling those babies is probably conducting an IQ test on a random sample of the populace.

TO DO AND SEE

PART ONE: TRUE OR FALSE

1. A nervous breakdown and a power outage have much in common.
2. Ohm's Law is merely a suggestion.
3. There's something seriously wrong with our dependence on electrical appliances. (Hint: They are both expensive and destructive to our bodies. Who has muscle tone anymore? Open a *National Geographic* and look at the muscle tone on the natives of Africa. Do they have electrical appliances? Of course not.)
4. When in doubt, do nothing.
5. If you have to stand somewhere while working on a broken electrical fixture, don't stand in a puddle.
6. Electrons hate us, and use the element of surprise to their advantage when attacking us.
7. It's a terrible thing to lose your mind or not to have a mind.

PART TWO: BRACE YOURSELF FOR A GRIM FUTURE BY ASKING YOURSELF THE FOLLOWING QUESTIONS:

8. What would the neighbors do if I sublet my house to a motorcycle gang? Would I feel responsible if property values in the neighborhood dropped?
9. If I posed as a CIA agent and took secret pictures of my neighbors' houses, then ran away if I were caught in the act, and spray-painted "We know where you live and what you're doing" on their driveways, what would be their probable reaction? What would my reaction to their reaction be?
10. The Greek playwright Aristophanes was killed in a freak accident when an eagle dropped a turtle on his head. Could modern housing techniques have saved his life? Discuss.
11. If you were to put a back porch on the Acropolis would you use: (a) dry wall? (b) plywood? (c) foamcore? (d) slabs of marble?

PART THREE: TOUGH ONES

12. Buy a half-gallon of cheap bourbon, drive to the middle of the desert nearest you, and stop. Get out of the car and remove your shoes. Now set fire to both your shoes and your vehicle. Barefoot, with only the bourbon to fortify you, try to make your way back to so-called civilization.
13. If the world is your oyster are you: (a) a bottom-feeder? (b) a normal Jane or Joe with normal desires? (c) "some kind of nut"? (d) all of the above?

14. Buy a nice home in a good neighborhood. Paint it a fluorescent orange that literally glows in the dark. Go door to door and solicit your neighbors' opinions on your decor. Now sit down with your family and ask them what they think.
15. Hitchhike around the country and get your head together. Have you done this? What's your next step? (a) Write a book. (b) Become a travel consultant. (c) Become a singer/songwriter with a small following in Massachusetts college towns. (d) Develop a line of vacation wear.
16. When we draw attention to the personal failings of those nearest and dearest to us, we often say things like "There's a wall between us, Joe" or "You're nothing but an empty shell, Jane." Which of the following terms from the construction industry could also be usefully appropriated by the pseudo-Science we call psychology?
    (a) Coping joint (b) Blueprint (c) Building inspector (d) Lapis lazuli (e) Oxy-acetylene flame (f) Paint remover (g) Plinth (h) Hammer (i) Staggered stud partition (j) Sandpaper (k) Rubble (l) Straight edge (m) Veneer (n) Zoning (o) Butt hinge (p) Bricklayer (q) Foreman (r) Joiner (s) Caulking (t) Screw (u) Cement (v) Bolt (w) Retarded hemihydrate plaster

2

PAYING THROUGH THE NOSE

LIVE THE FANTASY!

You might hang your mailbox in front of a Ralph Lauren–influenced concoction in the breadloaf hills of California, or a hastily built split level in a housing development in the Sunbelt. You may find yourself cheerfully gluing ethylene propylene diene monomer or some other elastomeric membrane to the leaky roof of a fixer-upper in Connecticut; you may even find yourself in the basement of your stately family home in Iowa, your breath forming clouds as you try to burn away the icicles that have formed on the water pipes with an oxy-acetylene torch.

These are the dubious joys of home-dwelling that have such a hypnotic hold on our psyches. Even as you read this, thousands of house-hopefuls are cruising the perimeters of the area in which they now live, real estate brochures and the classified section of newspapers strewn about them in the car. They have circled grainy, smeared photographs of houses with yellow markers. Every time they see the words Open House they experience a terrible spurt of adrenaline. Their minds are swimming in a word-salad sea: crpts, lndry, bdrms, lg yd, nr trns, fplc. . . . Vowels have disappeared from their lives! "Thr!" Mom shouts, stabbing at a map. "Trn hr!" Dad spins the wheel and sends the Volvo to a screeching halt in the driveway of the model home. Red, white, blue, and yellow banners flap gently in the breeze. A neatly groomed man and woman, with grins as bright as the brass buttons on their blue blazers, step out of the simulated-oak front door, and stride briskly forward to meet you. Could this be it? Could this be the starter home of your dreams?

Perhaps you've grown so excited by the preceding paragraph you've thrown this book aside with a cry and are even now striding through the Laundromats of your fair city, gathering smudged real estate brochures in your arms. Come back, I urge you. Scrub that smeared newsprint off your hands and sit back down. I know you're chomping (or champing, if you want to get technical about it) at the bit, but before we go on even a cursory tour of a house, you must reacquaint yourself with the one thing necessary to any home-dweller, whether renter or owner—money.

LEGAL TENDER

This is the grease that keeps the rat race running. The correct phrase for our currency is *legal tender*, but strangely enough, official measurement of the degree of tenderness for the coin of the realm does not fall on the U.S. Department of Agriculture, but the Food and Drug Administration.

Yes, our government considers money to be a drug. Before a coin or bill can leave the mint, it must first be tested on laboratory animals. Coins are fed to albino rats, who eventually become deranged and are "terminated with extreme prejudice," as the feds put it. Bills are given to chimpanzees, who take them to posh animal hotels and throw them around like water. They eventually become uncontrollable, arrogant bores and are sent to a special holding center beneath the White House, where they dictate foreign policy.

Money itself, you see, is relatively unimportant to John and Jane Citizen. What is important is the *threat* of money, a veiled hint that cash can be produced at a moment's notice, if it should come to that. Of course, it never will come to that. Only crack dealers and convenience-store clerks need cash. Cash is almost useless! Otherwise how do you explain why gasoline prices go to the tenth of a cent? We don't even have a coin that small! For most of us, the mere insinuation of capital is sufficient. This is called your *credit rating*.

If your credit rating is high enough, you may be able to obtain a *loan*. This means that a bank, or similar banklike institution, will back you up if you should desire to drop even bigger hints about your cash on hand, with the provision that you must be worth twice as much as the amount they are willing to give you.

To make a long story short, if you want to live anywhere, you must first bankrupt yourself. You must accumulate massive debt and assets up the wazoo (see page 40) before you can even think of stepping over the threshold of your future home. This is most quickly accomplished through the use of credit cards.

CREDIT CARDS

These are slim pieces of laser-encoded plastic used to purchase unnecessary objects from mail-order catalogues or television info-mercials. Objects purchased through a mail-order or toll-free number don't exist in the universe as we know it. They exist in a hypothetical universe—a parallel universe if you will, which largely resembles a railroad yard packed with warehouses. These warehouses, unlike Plato's cave, are empty. The objects don't exist until you desire them. When you phone in your credit card number for, let's say, the Time/Life home-repair collection, a process occurs in these warehouses that very much resembles dreaming. These objects, based on your need and good credit, literally will themselves into existence, and eventually to your door. This process takes four to six weeks, unless the company goes out of business, which involves a different process Science calls "kissing your money good-bye."

The fact that you need credit to live somewhere, yet you must live somewhere before you can be given credit, would seem to put citizens in a double bind. Yet, oddly, the system works. It is only in our psyche that the pain of contradictions is truly felt. Going into debt is a hideous responsibility, for which no adult has been adequately prepared! Nobody told you that when credit cards expire, so does the economy.

BANKING HOURS

It is obvious then that *theoretical* money, not *actual* money, makes the world go around. So what happens when the banks are closed on Sundays?

To put it simply, the earth loses momentum. The pull of people trying to wrench goods and services away from others is the force which keeps our planet spinning. With more transactions taking place entirely on paper, and nothing actually changing hands, the earth has slowed appreciably—particularly in the past decade with the innovation of junk bonds. Junk bonds are actually "anti-money." If enough junk bonds are issued, the earth could conceivably spin backwards. To help stop that slowing, automatic teller machines were invented to keep money moving twenty-four hours a day, seven days a week.

FULL-TIME DEBT MANAGEMENT

Our economy is so arranged that opportunities to spend frivolously and spend often are everywhere. The shopping mall, of course, is the opportunity most thrown our way. The next time you go to Oakwood Hills, Hillwood Oaks, Oakhill Woods, or your local equivalent, go to one of the directories listing the various shops. You will see an *X* that says "You are here."

How do they know?

It will shock you to learn that today's shopping mall is a highly interactive environment. Computers analyze every aspect of each prospective customer who enters the mall. Every time you ride an escalator you are weighed to see how much lighter or heavier you are than the last time you rode. The measurements are accurate enough to detect the amount of money you have left in your billfold or the precise cost of the merchandise you've purchased. When you grip the escalator's handrail, it measures your CDL, or Consumer Desperation Level, which in turn determines which subliminal message will be directed at you from the hidden subwoofers in the ceiling. Yes, pinpointing your location is just the tip of the iceberg.

Sometimes our leisure habits and the subliminal demands of our consumer culture get the better of us, and we truly shop till we drop. How many times, for example, have you heard someone complain of being down to his or her "last red cent?" Believe me, this red cent is all too real.

No, the government does not mint scarlet pennies. The coin in question is a secret membership emblem for Over-Spenders Anonymous. Avowed over-spenders carry this coin with them at all times. If this is the last coin they possess, and they feel the urge to spend it, they lick it first. The cyanide coating that gives the cent its distinctive color will do its deadly work before the sale can be transacted. So when you hear shoppers talk about being down to that lethal coin, it's really a cry for help. Lend them money immediately, or have them committed. Circumstances will vary.

FYI...

The wazoo is the portion of the anatomy that holds an excess of anything, in anticipation of further use. Like the camel's hump or the kangaroo's pouch, the human's wazoo developed as an adaptation for survival. In primitive man, the wazoo was located at the base of the spine, much like the "butt pack" we see today. Over time it has appeared in different areas of the anatomy, including behind the knees and on that little ridge beneath the nose and above the upper lip. In modern man the wazoo is merely a metaphor to most of us, unless we have something to hide, in which case it's usually a Swiss bank account.

RECREATION

If you're even mildly agoraphobic, there are more subtle ways to throw your money away than buying shoddy goods in a vast shopping structure crowded with glassy-eyed bargain hunters. Why not give recreation a try?

As the structure of the word suggests, re-creation involves playing God. Human nature demands that the only way we can really enjoy ourselves is through puffing ourselves up to positions of over-importance. Hence the desire to rebuild all creation, to make all things new. Of course we lack the power to accomplish this, but many of us have fun trying. Again, this is the Roy of the spirit wrestling with the Dale, the *carefree* Bob making a flip remark at the expense of *stick-in-the-mud* Bob, to the laughter and applause of an unseen studio audience.

So the emotional hangover can be quite severe. That is why recreational drugs are no longer in vogue.

On television, our models for behavior seem reluctant to leave the house. The primary reason for this is economic. It's cheaper to show Dad Brady and the gang interacting in their studio-built home than to lug nine actors, a dog, their retinue and crew to a shopping mall. It's much more cost-effective to show Bob returning to his swinging bachelor pad, overnight bag in hand, than to fly everybody to Tahiti. Grips, gaffers, and camera operators seldom get to go to Tahiti. This is why so many television crews are cranky and irritable. But it's also why television producers always seem so jovial. The money saved by staying in one location allows them to make house payments in Beverly Hills. And once the cameras stop rolling they can go to Tahiti any damn time they feel like it.

No wonder the rest of us slump in our easy chairs at home, remote control in hand. A word of caution is definitely in order: Recreation, like shopping, should be left to those constitutionally able to handle it. If you think you're one of them, read on.

VISITING OTHERS

Although most in the Scientific community eschew social contact, many non-Scientists seem to derive a sick pleasure from visiting their peers. This is to be encouraged so long as the costs to society do not outweigh the benefits.

There are certain human interactions that can only take place in person. It is hard to fax your affection to someone. To digitize emotion is to diminish its efficacy.

As any one of my ex-wives can attest, it is extremely difficult to carry on a long-term relationship without personal contact. In a way, one becomes mated to the creature or device one spends the most time with. In that sense, I have been married to a certain cyclotron since 1953. This far exceeds the duration of any of my so-called marriages.

Visits should be kept brief and businesslike, although with a certain casual air. Information need not be given emphatically; indeed, there is a certain charm in circumlocution and getting to the point as indirectly as possible.

This is often called chewing the rag, schmoozing, or talking, and should not be confused with lecturing or defending a thesis.

Under no circumstances, when visiting others, should you accept a drink of anything but distilled water. Many a great mind has left this dimension thanks to a rewarmed cup of coffee that was brewed some time ago.

THEATER

If you're looking for an exotic way to get rid of disposable income, there's sure to be everything from a Neil Simon play to a quivering performance artist somewhere near you. Believe it or not, the theater does still exist in our culture, though it mostly thrives as an educational exercise or as a showcase for actors hoping to find work in Hollywood.

How does live performance survive when our entire popular culture is focused on the tube and the multiplex screen? Some people are simply too expansive to be so encapsulated: Their voices are too loud; they aren't good looking enough; when they act they don't act "natural," they act like, well, actors.

These people need jobs too. Sure, they could find employment as camp counselors and motivational speakers, but opportunities in those areas are limited. On the other hand, if we ignore the needs of those who break into song at the drop of a hat, who think tap dancing is as noble an occupation as computer programming, then we will have far less unemployment, substance abuse, and people seeking new careers as travel agents and Realtors.

The next time you're forced to writhe in embarrassment as you watch a thin, naked woman shout insults at her absent mother through a bullhorn, or watch your local barber complain about trouble in River City, remember that these people could be out causing real trouble. Seen in this light, your support of theater becomes an act of mercy, earning you not only good feeling and much-needed self-esteem, but karmic abundance.

STAND-UP COMEDY

Speaking of live performance, there was a time not so long ago when well-dressed couples could dine in elegance and take in a floor show featuring lovely women, a swooning *chanteuse* or two, and a hot jazz combo. Today the only things nightclubs offer are two-drink minimums and comics.

In general, there is nothing more tragic than a standup comedian. Only by examining a stand-up's compulsion for public humiliation can we hope to understand why one would pursue a career for which he or she is so ill-suited.

Just as Jerry Lewis hopes to attain culture by hoodwinking the French into thinking he is an artist, so does Steve Allen pose as a TV intellectual, an oxymoron if ever there was one. What prompts someone to broadcast to the world the limits of his ability?

Actors act, writers write, teachers teach. Stand-up comedians cry out for attention and pity. Even more mystifying is the tendency of a certain segment of the populace to pay admission to a so-called comedy club. These people possess both sadistic and masochistic tendencies.

For what can cause your stomach to knot more quickly than a comic, desperate for laughs, making distorted fart noises too loudly into a microphone?

Yet for every drop of anguished sweat in the audience, the comic is sweating buckets. For every frayed nerve in the house, onstage there is a complete nervous breakdown.

Gone are the days when an evening at a nightclub meant dignified waiters with pencil-thin moustaches, a gleaming dance floor, and attractive women selling cigarettes. Now it is a painfully intense glimpse of the true and horrible face of human despair. Save your money.

THE MOVIES

It may be that *Aliens*[3] was the first Hollywood movie whose protagonist's head had been shaved not in a display of chic (*à la* Telly Savalas or Yul Brynner) but purely to control lice. This admirable cinematic salute to hygiene, however, is the only bright spot in today's depressing cultural climate. Film itself has become disturbing. Let's look back at random.

- *Home Alone*. A boy abandoned by his family mutilates stupid intruders.
- *Total Recall*. A cheerful working stiff gradually realizes he's really an evil corporate spy from Mars.
- *Robocop*. A crime-fighting cyborg gradually realizes he's really a formerly dead policeman resurrected by an evil corporation.
- *Ghost*. A yuppie gradually realizes he's really dead.
- *Hook*. A yuppie gradually realizes he's really Peter Pan.
- *Jurassic Park*. An elderly gentleman realizes it's a bad idea to clone dinosaurs.

I could go on, but since I haven't seen any of these movies, I probably should be cautious in my judgments. I only view films Scientifically, on my LCD wrist monitor. As far as I know, no Hollywood movie is available in liquid crystal. As a matter of fact, I believe I possess the only two movies in the world available in the format (see Appendix).

If Hollywood starts making movies in 200 mm you might catch me in a theater again, but not until. If I'm going to shell out ten dollars for a movie, it had better be on a screen the size of four city blocks.

But that's not the point. The point is there appears to be a common denominator among the modern blockbusters, and that is the theme of *amnesia*. The family in *Home Alone* can't *remem-*

ber where they put their child. Arnold can't *remember* that he's evil. The richest man in the world can't *remember* where Beverly Hills is.

Can this be more proof (if more is needed) of my Two Bobs theory? Robert Reed can't *remember* that he used to be carefree Bob Cummings. All across America, Tamaras have forgotten they used to be Tammys; Susans are feeling the lack of Suzies in their psyches; Stevens, Michaels, and Margarets are in a state of denial about Steve, Mike, Maggie, Margie, Marggie, Peg, Gretchen, Gretl, or Peggy, as the case may be.

Is Hollywood's sudden infatuation with amnesia subtle propaganda, an insidious campaign to keep America complacent in the face of danger? Have we become a nation of amnesiacs lost and alone in a toxic and hazardous environment? I'm no film critic, but I have to say yes.

FAMILY OUTINGS

Many family-oriented sites are reasonably priced or even free. You can take the kids swimming in a scum-ridden pond, or drag them for a stroll through a drug-dealer infested park, gratis. Family picnics are always free, if you think having your offspring see your worthless brother, their uncle, pound down one too many brewskis and start screaming at his parents, their grandparents, that they never really loved him, bears no cost.

No, you're going to have to shell out some money. If you still want to keep an eye on the pocketbook, there's the zoo—but that's really just an overgrown farm with gerenuks and dik-diks in lieu of cattle and sheep. If you've seen one spider monkey, frankly, you've seen them all.

Also cheap are those hands-on Science museums that are springing up all over the place. These museums, be forewarned, are content with the mere tricks of Science—optical illusions, bubbles, crystal formation, and such. There's nothing wrong with that, of

course. But I've never seen any staff members issuing formaldehyde and pointy sticks to youngsters at the admissions gate, then commanding them to pith away at a floor crawling with amphibians. Next time you go to one of these museums, check out the friendly staff. They're all wearing T-shirts that say "The Friendly Science Center Kid Place For Growing." Not a lab smock in the bunch. Need I say more?

Traditional museums, on the other hand, are just gigantic closets with art in one and stuffed giraffes in another. I am a great admirer of the taxidermist's art, but in order to appreciate a diorama of the delicate ecosystem of life on the pampas, one must have a certain maturity, a certain *gravitas*, that children lack.

Besides, you must remember, the function of the outing is to throw your money away. For this, nothing beats the giant theme park. When it comes to vacation fun, there's a small window of joy open only to kids aged ten, who actually seem to get pleasure from loud noises, exploding lights, and machines that spin them around until they get sick to their stomachs. But even their brief window of pleasure is somewhat blurred by their natural hyperactivity, and soon the window will dissolve altogether into a wall of peer pressure, boredom, and embarrassment by other family members.

But that doesn't matter. What matters is, you're throwing money away by the wallet- and purseful. Ultimately it all will end as it always does—with you and your family stumbling in the darkness through a vast parking lot, casting up tiny pebbles with your flip-flops, as the sunburned flesh of your thighs and upper arms glows softly under the vapor lamps. Into the Cherokee! And so to dreamland.

TRAVEL

And what about the lure of the open road? Do we still feel it? Or do only the retired among us haul themselves into the RV and tool down Route 66? Where are the Wild Ones today? The Neal Cassadys and Kerouacs?

Once we put Saint Christopher in our rear windows to aid us on our journey. Thanks to ecumenicalism, this saint has been replaced by stuffed animals. We place these behind us in vehicles we neither wanted nor desired, traveling toward destinations at which we would rather not arrive. When we see a sign saying SPEED ZONE, we *slow down*! When we see a sign proclaiming, "Don't even think of parking here," we try desperately to think of something else. Such are our modern lives.

FYI...

You may have noticed that the windshield wiper on the driver's side always wears out first. Until recently, Science didn't know why.

First of all, it seems that rain doesn't cause windshield wiper wear. Instead invisible (yet very real) rays emanate from a driver's eyes, causing the wipers to wear out. Swatting those rays is a tough job, and the wiper rubber tends to fray along the edges, especially if the driver is irritable and producing rays more caustic than usual.

Sometimes, given the presence of a backseat driver, the passenger wiper can wear at an equal rate, but this condition is rare, and only occurs if the driver is as serene as the passenger is irritable. One way to prolong the life of your wiper blades is to wear dark glasses while driving. These block the rays but also inhibit vision, something you don't want after dark, or during a rain storm. The best solution is, as always, prevention. *Have your wiper blades replaced at least once a week.*

Keeping all this in mind, remember it's not as important as where you're going, and/or why.

Science has finally admitted it doesn't really know how long a parsec is, even though it's been measuring the darn things for years. There are reasons for this. For one thing, the European parsec is significantly shorter than the American parsec. Also, Europeans use metersticks to measure theirs, while Americans use yardsticks. It's also very difficult to get a parsec to lie still long enough to be measured accurately, and the slime they exude when frightened only adds to the confusion. Throw in the fact that a parsec bite can be life-threatening, and you can see why most Scientists are satisfied with a "guesstimate." And, after all, in the great scheme of things, what does it all matter?

REAL ESTATE

We must admit to ourselves that all of our purchases and travel time are just ways Americans have developed to stave off the inevitable step of purchasing a home. Carefully then, let us broach the subject of real estate.

Unlike the human orgasm, real estate is, as its name implies, very real. Once we ignore the petty difference between existence and nonexistence, we find that real estate and sexuality are basically the same thing.

Human sexuality is a system of incentives and regulations governing the most fundamental of physical transactions, and the most personal of personal properties. On the other hand, a buyer with shaky credit uses a balloon mortgage to purchase a love shack; a seller dreaming of a career in real estate finds his or her balloon popped by the harsh pinprick of economic reality.

This is not to suggest that you must have sex with your Realtor in order to arrive as a homeowner. Sex with a Realtor is theoretically possible, of course, but will not help you buy real estate with little or no money down—one of the highest aspirations of any American, as anyone who watches television can tell you.

No, you cannot have it both ways. Either you subscribe to a world of free love and unwashed hippies or the grim ascetism of the marketplace. One cannot afford to fool oneself about true value. Either a home is priced to sell or it remains forever on the market. Either the roof leaks or it doesn't. Fidelity in marriage finds its equivalent in the prompt loan payment and regular upkeep of the property.

WHAT DO YOU BELIEVE ABOUT REAL ESTATE?

Chances are you're afraid of your home. Whether you rent or own it, whether it's a palace or a one-room hovel, your home exerts a disturbing influence over your every thought. This is because wo/man is, by his or her very nature, nomadic. You have no business living in one place for more than a few weeks.

Our forefathers knew this. They heard that highway sound all the time. They wore their rambling shoes, and carried all their belongings in a dirty bandana that hung, like an overripe tomato, on the end of a stick.

Though not a real Science, anthropology tells us that our hobo ancestors were hunter/gatherers. This is an anthropological euphemism for what we now call street people. Like Porgy, they had "plenty o' nothin'." But were they happy?

Interestingly, there exists a primitive demographic survey done by the Niilsoens (the Scottish clan who invented the cellular phone, around A.D. 555). Whenever they pillaged a hamlet, they always placed a booth on the far side of the invasion point, to poll those lucky enough to flee. Of course, those who gave answers displeasing to the Niilsoens would be put to the sword, so the data are flawed, but they do give a picture of insanely happy races (see Niilsoen Exit Poll in Appendix). Based on those ancient documents, we can safely say that housing in the sixth century was just one more thing for visiting warriors to put to the torch. Our ancestors would have been better off cowering under a bush. Are we any better today?

WHAT KIND OF PERSON BECOMES A REALTOR, ANYWAY?

We might as well ask ourselves this question right now before wasting any more time trying to unscramble the tangled web of mixed messages, innuendo, and just plain nonsense that accompanies even cursory contact with a Realtor.

Chances are the persons who insist on driving you to show a property only three blocks from your home are, first of all, painfully lonely. They were always the last to be picked as team members or dance partners, the ones to whom it was explained, "I'm sorry, but there's not enough to go around . . . could you make do with this instead?'' They responded through hot tears of shame and rage, ''Yes . . . No problem.'' Of such is the person who grew up to be a Realtor.

So here you are, captive in the car of a psychically scarred individual who hopes selling you a home will lead to wholeness again. You're already in a terrible position, and the longer you let this go on the worse your position will be. Remember this: It's not your problem. Realtors are sick. If they want to change, only they can change themselves.

Alas, the cruel fact is, no one can make a Realtor whole again, because the Realtor was never whole to begin with. Always on the outside looking in, the Realtor has come to believe that by selling homes he or she will find a home. Logically, this makes no sense, but then Real Estate is not a logical discipline. It is, like its cousins Advertising and Mail Fraud, based on the crass manipulation of human emotion.

You must act decisively and firmly. Delay will only make things more painful. Even if it means throwing yourself out of your Realtor's moving car, it's worth it! Of course, it wouldn't hurt to ask the Realtor to pull over, but if the Realtor won't comply, shove open the door and hurl yourself onto the pavement.

TO DO AND SEE

1. Purchase a hidden wireless microphone from a spy supply store (check the Yellow Pages for the one nearest you). Plant this on your significant other, and monitor his or her daily affairs from afar. Be sure to carry a tape recorder with you as well, to keep a permanent record of the most interesting segments. Store these tapes in a safe place for future use when circumstances warrant.
2. Obtain blank legal forms from your local courthouse and begin to sue everyone you come in contact with. At least a small percentage of your potential litigants will opt to settle out of court, bringing you both financial gain and a sense of empowerment. If you can't win

the title of Best Loved member of the community, at least you can be Most Feared.

3. Build a bunker in your basement. Now that the threat of Soviet nuclear attack has largely disappeared, people are becoming complacent and letting their supplies of crackers and water deteriorate. Now is the time to pick up bunker building supplies and food stocks for a fraction of their former cost! Be sure to include a short-wave radio, and a generous cache of firearms and ammunition. You can never be too careful, especially when you're projecting negativity all around you. Remember, the law of karma demands that you get back what you send out, so get ready!

Contusions and abrasions heal in a matter of weeks, but a thirty-year fixed mortgage can take an eternity to pay off, especially if you're forced to refinance to fix the roof.

WHICH BOB ARE YOU?

BOB	BOB
Robert Cummings	Robert Reed
David Letterman	Jay Leno
Cher	Sonny
Roy	Dale
Race car driver	Bus driver
Madonna	Annette Funicello
Actor	Bodyguard
Baseball player	Golfer
Highway patrol	LAPD
Partridge Family	Brady Bunch
Patty Lane	Cathy Lane
Gilligan	The Skipper
Della Street	Perry Mason
Flipper	Lassie
Seven Dwarfs	Snow White
Dummy	Ventriloquist
Riggs	Murtaugh
Arnold	Sly
Godzilla	King Kong
Katharine Hepburn	Joan Crawford
Robert DeNiro	Bob Newhart
Nat Cole Trio	Nat "King" Cole
Batman	Superman
Holmes	Watson
Espresso	Decaf

3

EMPLOYMENT WOES

OUR DWINDLING WORLD

What have you learned so far? Not enough to deter you from the path of home-dwelling, I'm sure. Not that I want to dissuade you from having a roof over your head; far from it. But America doesn't seem to realize that the piper we call shelter has a price. We have seen the price we pay—worthless goods (like overpriced inflatable foot-care systems from the mall), popular culture, a squelched urge to wander, and that special anxiety about the debt that, paradoxically, is necessary to purchase a home in the first place.

Before we can even begin to explore the wonders and terrors of the home, we must first generate income. QED. This means work. Jobs. Employment.

THE OUTLOOK

Despite deregulation, we are still overregulated. It now takes five men to monitor the work of one. These inspectors are, of course, paid far more than the one they are to supervise. Fifty years ago, it took a hundred laborers to erect a building or build a road. Today, that same job would take three workers; fifteen to twenty supervisors, inspectors, consultants, and specialists; and a half-million-dollar machine to do the work the other seventy-five people would have done if they'd been given the chance. Instead, those folks are on public assistance, or back in school learning to be substance-abuse counselors. That's the price we pay for progress. And it makes the job of jobseeking tough.

THE INTERVIEW

JOBSEEKER

When you're being interviewed for a job, it's best to take an aggressive, upbeat attitude. Come in ready to mount an offensive against your interviewer. Demand to know the full range of benefits in addition to salary. If you find the salary offering pitiful, say so. This will create the impression that you are a grizzled veteran of the employment marketplace, and no one to trifle with.

It doesn't hurt to dress in a brash, highly individual manner. It shows that you stand out from the crowd, that you're not a follower, but a trendsetter.

Loud, forceful displays of burping and farting only further this devil-may-care countenance. Employers like to know that they're dealing with a self-starter, a motivated employee who won't constantly be waiting for guidance. Again, blowing your nose onto your shirttail only reinforces this impression of a rugged individualist with total disregard for others' sense of propriety.

EMPLOYER

You've got to see just how much the jobseeker wants the job. You can afford to be tough. After all, there are ten thousand people applying for the position. As you look out the window of your corner office you can see the line stretching away for blocks. When the prospective employee enters the office, ignore him or her. Just stand, staring grimly out the window, or if you're at your desk, frown at the telephone and tap your fingers.

Let two minutes pass in silence. When you finally choose to speak, tell the employee, in a highly accusatory tone, that you run a nonsmoking office and you have zero tolerance for drug abuse. If the job hopeful is a woman, ask her bluntly if she's pregnant. If he's a man, tell him if he's hired, the company will be his family, and if he can't deal with that, there's the door.

Find nonexistent spelling errors in the applicant's résumé. Stare at the applicant's chest, make a face, and ask, "What *is* that you're wearing?" Challenge each person to an arm-wrestling match.

Finally, you must be certain that employees will respond to your management style. To ensure that they can take it, place your face inches from each applicant, then scream hoarsely and incoherently, your face purple with rage, veins bulging from your neck.

This makes for a grueling interview process, but whether it's for an executive vice-presidency or a custodial position, it's the only way to get the worker you desire.

ON THE JOB

Of course, once you get the job, that's just the beginning of your troubles. You'll find yourself plagued by heartless supervisors, uncooperative colleagues, and ruthless competitors. What's worse, things will disappear mysteriously from your desk: pens, paper, and staplers prime among them. Most serious of all, you will find yourself walking around the office holding a coffee cup and suddenly discover it's gone.

The cause of this, Science now knows, is that full employment invariably leads to Roget's Syndrome. Named after Henri Roget, the famed French paleontologist, Roget's Syndrome causes sufferers to hurl objects unconsciously into another dimension. With most sufferers these objects are very small, usually the caps of ballpoint pens and house keys, but in advanced cases of Roget's, the objects tend to get much larger. Medical literature notes that Andrew the Horrible, the Russian ruler of the fourteenth century, actually tossed his castle and estate into this dimension. Naturally, the law of conservation of energy and mass demands that these objects still exist—and they do, in that hidden dimension which may or not be ruled over by the late Rod Serling.

FAXING

One of the joys of the workspace, besides creating zany memos and making photocopies of your private parts, is the opportunity to see if you can fax yourself.

To save you the trouble, I'll tell you you can. But it really, really hurts. You must also have a dedicated phone line to fax a living object; that is, if you want it to be alive when it reaches the other end. I have a fiber optic cable about three feet in diameter. When I tested the system by faxing myself around the globe ten times, I suffered only minor fax lag. But when I thought of the money I'd saved in air fares, it was worth it.

The real pain comes when you're first transmitted into the system. You know that annoying warbling tone that happens at the start of a fax? That's the sound of the so-called Fax Chompers reducing the document to bits and bytes of information. Fortunately, the whole process takes less than a minute, even for a three-hundred-pounder like me.

If you choose to fax yourself, I recommend reciting tables of natural logarithms to distract yourself. That and plenty of ibuprofen make it bearable.

WORK-RELATED HEALTH ISSUES

I bring up the above to point out that even aspects of a job that appear at first glance to be pluses—if you're allowed to drink coffee at your desk or transmit your body halfway around the world via fax—are actually minuses. Yes, whether you're a prostitute or a congressman, every job eventually leads to illness.

Many choose to ignore the messages their bodies give them regarding hunger, fatigue, instinctual drives, and emotion. (As a Scientist, I confess, I find I just don't have the time to deal with such nonessentials: If it doesn't advance research, I don't have the patience for it.)

Ignoring the danger signs works well for a while, but with age comes vulnerability, and eventually the circuit breakers flip and the system shuts down. Fortunately, the human body contains no reset button. If it did we would be like nuclear power plant workers who override a system's safety circuits until a major meltdown occurs.

How can you protect yourself against total malfunction? Contrary to popular belief, an apple a day won't keep the doctor away. Nothing can keep a doctor away if he's determined to get you. (Eating apples, however, will keep lawyers away, if you can convince them that the reason you're eating apples is that you can't afford steak.) The following warning signs could help you avoid voiding your own warranty.

RUNNY NOSE, ITCHY EYES

These are often the external symptoms of an internal disorder such as Elvis worship, or belief in a personal relationship with UFOs.

Over-the-counter medications offer some relief, but it's far better simply to stop believing in obvious falsehoods.

HABITUAL NEGATIVE THINKING

Although it is not uncommon to find yourself stuck in a painful mental rut, there is an easy way out—and up. Simply take a bath in a solution of vinegar and baking soda. The bubbles are stimulating, and the vinegar cleans the largest organ, the skin, of any clogging soap scum.

BEDWETTING

The simplest cure for bedwetting is to sleep standing up. Bedwetting itself indicates unresolved early childhood conflicts about toy possession and unexpressed desires to have an open marriage.

CONVERSION EXPERIENCES

In our perpetual desire to be special, many of us allow our egos to overstep their natural boundaries. Then we begin to "buy" our own delusions. No relief can be obtained unless we are willing to beat our egos back into submission. This can be done through self-flagellation and other acts of auto-induced humiliation.

PRIAPISM

Another side effect of Elvis worship and UFO abduction.

FOOT ODOR

Easily treated by bathing in vinegar and baking soda (see Habitual Negative Thinking, above). Some people produce foot odor that strongly resembles certain popular colognes. These people can sell their dirty socks to perfume manufacturers. Check with your friends to see if you belong in this group. It could be your ticket to self-employment and an early retirement.

So you see, the home can perform a useful function, helping you keep your health so you can work at your job to pay for the home. Taking care of yourself while maintaining this vicious cycle isn't all that hard, provided you're not so consumed with self-loathing that it goes against your every instinct. These simple actions, taken every day (on a daily basis, to put it Scientifically), provide the foundation of so-called normal living, which the rest of the world has been engaged in since the dawn of time. Don't feel bad that you've just become aware of them. After all, you've been preoccupied with your work.

ON-THE-JOB SHRINKAGE

If you were to scan your image at a very high resolution and store it on a hard disk, then process it in PageMaker and print it out on a laser printer, you might be able to change those aspects of your personality that cause you the most trouble, especially the compulsion to wear stripes with plaids and any phobia involving running water or aftershave lotion.

It's all part of the exciting new field of computerized auto-psychiatry. They say it's all the rage in Europe, but has yet to catch on in this country. This probably has something to do with the pressure the American Psychiatric Association has put on the leading computer makers to nip this thing in the bud. I've heard some pretty favorable stories of computer-enhanced personality improvement.

Some people even credit the process with the transformation of the Soviet Union. But those people are idiots.

ONE FINAL TIP

Ever since the advent of television, the American Medical Association has urged us to see our doctor every six months. Soon the dentists were right behind them, with the same stern suggestion. The American Psychiatric Institute is probably going to be next, along with podiatrists, chiropractors, and phrenologists. If that's how you want to spend your money, fine. But whenever I need a little TLC, I stick my head in the target end of a linear accelerator. The visuals are tremendous, and even though my hair falls out for a few weeks, it grows back as silky soft and shiny as an old pair of pants.

ALTERNATIVE MEDICINE: AN EXCLUSIVE INTERVIEW WITH DR. SCIENCE

This reporter interviewed Dr. Science in his underground laboratory, the Fortress of Arrogance. The self-proclaimed authority seemed aloof yet relaxed as we chatted in his living quarters, tucked just behind the cyclotron. Although Dr. Science often seemed irritated by the questions he was asked, he did answer many of them, and the knowledge we gleaned from the Supreme Expert (his words, not ours) is listed below.

Q. *Dr. Science, how are crystals used for healing?*

A. Scientists have long known that crystals generate invisible energy rays, which I call Gullibillium Rays, or G-rays. These rays come from molecules of pure hokum, which vibrate along the planes of fantasy. When these rays hit the third chakra of a true believer, the law of conservation of energy and mass is temporarily suspended and the believer is "healed." Although this process has been known since the Middle Ages, it has only recently risen to the level of a fad in America. Prices of crystals have soared in recent years, and will continue to rise, until another fad fills the void in American consciousness.

Q. *What is iridology?*

A. Iridology is the study of the iris of the human eye. The supporting theory states that the human iris is actually a relative of the iris plant. Even as we speak, Scientists are attempting to grow human irises in a test tube environment. Picture, if you will, this table setting: a bowl with a human iris floating in the middle! What a conversation piece!

Q. *I've heard a lot about hands-on healing lately. Is this something new?*

A. On the contrary, it's as old as organized crime. The term *hands-on* refers to the healer's ability to determine the size of the patient's wallet before the so-called healing session begins. This laying on of hands determines the length of treatment, which roughly corresponds to the fatness of the wallet.

At this point Dr. Science strayed from the Q&A format and began to pace back and forth, talking very rapidly. Fortunately, this reporter was able to capture the discourse on a variable-speed tape recorder and play the contents back at a slower speed.

Medicine, like professional wrestling, has many diverse factions. In wrestling, we have had some very large figures such as Andre the Giant and Hulk Hogan. In medicine, we have celebrities like Dr. Christiaan Barnard and Dr. Ruth, a superstar in her own right and deserving of unending media attention.

These alternative therapies hit a holistic hole-in-one in their careful disregard of the established norms of conventional medicine. They achieve this by using kundalini energy.

Unlike electrical energy, kundalini energy is free and nonpolluting.

There is a tiny kundalini energy generator inside each of us, located just above the fifth chakra, or belly button as the nonmystics call it.

Under normal conditions, kundalini energy is invisible. But during times of extreme stress, or if the observer happens to be wearing polarized glasses, purple streams of kundalini energy can be seen streaming from the midsections of those around us.

At this point a viewer might begin to question his/her sanity and the very nature of reality. Don't freak out. This is normal. It's normal for us to be deeply frightened by purple streams emanating from belly buttons.

Careful observers will note that there are some who seem to be using this energy to enhance their daily lives. Have you ever known someone who never seems to run out of gas? Someone who doesn't drink coffee, yet is always jittery? A fellow who is always running here and there and yet never seems to accomplish anything?

Chances are these people have found a way to tap into kundalini energy. Any Scientist in his right mind knows that Progress as we know it is impossible without tapping into that power source. Yet does using kundalini energy doom one to a life of mindless mysticism?

Fortunately, no. Fact is, many yogis are intellectually capable of grasping the concepts necessary to be a Scientist in the modern world.

Wernher von Braun, the Nazi wunderkind who helped launch America's space program, had so much kundalini energy in his body that he literally could not sit still. The chair behind his desk was actually a small trampoline. On the other hand, research has shown that Gandhi had almost no left-brain development. This is consistent with our theory that you can have kundalini energy all over the place, but still no real brainpower.

And what, you may ask, do Wernher von Braun, Joyce Brothers, and Hulk Hogan have in common? They all know more about kundalini energy than you do. That is why society pays them so well.

You must decide for yourself whether you will become a psychic healer or avail yourself of a healer's services. Or you can do as I do and ignore the issue altogether.

At this point the Supreme Expert stopped talking. Suddenly oblivious to the presence of this reporter, he turned his attentions to an exception-

ally foul-smelling experiment in progress. This reporter left, his exit unnoticed by Dr. Science.

JOBS AND YOU

No doubt you've heard the by now familiar phrase "You don't have to be a rocket Scientist" to know this or that. Or "Does it take a brain surgeon to figure this out?" Are rocket Scientists and brain surgeons really that smart?

Boy, are they! Rocket Scientists are not only brainy, they're often poets and musicians of awesome ability. Dr. Edward Teller was a colleague of Sylvia Plath and William Carlos Williams as well as a fine harpsichordist. Wernher von Braun played an excellent blues harp, and once spent half a year riding the rails with beats Jack Kerouac and Allen Ginsberg. Most rocket Scientists are recipients of the coveted MacArthur Foundation genius awards, and many are Mensa members as well. As for brain surgeons, their arrogance is matched only by their aptitude.

So what's the problem? Why aren't you running out right now to sign up with a rocket Scientist or brain surgeon training program? You probably know the answer to that as well as I do.

First of all we have a glut of rocket Scientists and brain surgeons. Motorcycle helmet laws and cutbacks at NASA have assured a long line of these eggheads in the unemployment line. And second of all, as the cliché phrases suggest, you *don't* have to be a rocket Scientist or brain surgeon to perform most of the tasks demanded by our society.

Just the other day, I was in a fast-food restaurant doing a French fry comparison for statistical purposes. The fellow ahead of me didn't like the way his hamburger had been cooked and said, sarcastically, "What, is it brain surgery to cook a hamburger?" Well, the fry cook ran out from behind the grill, trembling with rage, and said, "I *am* a brain surgeon."

Ironically, it turned out the sarcastic fellow was a rocket Scientist who'd spent his last dollar on that hamburger, so it all goes to show you it only pays to put on high-and-mighty airs if you have tenure, belong to a union, or you happen to be Dr. Science.

But still, the sad fact of the matter is, jobs are scarce, and we're picky. This is a dangerous combination. How do you decide which job is right for you? To save you some time, here's a brief checklist.

ANTHROPOLOGY

The anthropologist's job is to study the mores of primitive tribes in New Guinea. This can lead to tenure in many universities as well as PBS documentaries, but the job has its problems. There aren't that many primitive tribes *left* in New Guinea, and those few are already crawling with anthropologists. Some tribes have already put up signs saying "No anthropologists allowed." Other tribes have moved without leaving a forwarding address. All through New Guinea, packs of anthropologists tramp through the rain forests, calling out the names of primitive tribes in pathetic and forlorn voices cracking with weariness and frustration. You must ask yourself, Is it worth it?

Tools of the Trade

Jodhpurs, malaria pills, trinkets, hiking boots, waterproof notebook. Being French doesn't hurt.

ARCHAEOLOGY

Archaeologists crouch for hours in a sand pit under a blazing sun, chipping away at a two-thousand-year-old urn, while officials in

fezzes stand patiently above them awaiting bribes. Sounds like fun, doesn't it? But it too has its drawbacks.

The primary drawback, of course, is the so-called mummy's curse. This assures most archaeologists of a horrible death at the hands of a bandage-swathed zombie. Here again, you must decide if the glamour of the profession is really worth it.

Tools of the Trade

Little tiny pickax, tanna leaves, pith helmet, khaki shorts.

If you are a woman interested in this profession, being the incarnation of ''she-whom-the-ancients-call-Ayesha'' can go a long way toward ensuring your survival.

ASTRONOMY

The study of heavenly bodies has little practical value. Unless you're with NASA, astronomy just won't pay the rent.

Tools of the Trade

Liquid oxygen, telescope.

BIOLOGY

Under biology's gentle wing are nestled sub-Sciences like botany, zoology, and even ichthyology, which demands that you study fish. Bugs, birds, evolution—it's all grist for biology's mill. And biology tackles each messy job with glassy-eyed devotion.

I've always considered biology to be more a hobby than a profession. The new field of genetic manipulation might put some change in your pocket, but the rest of biology is kind of iffy, moneywise.

Tools of the Trade

Snake-bite kit, microscope, slides, labels, petri dish, those little pointy things you use to pith frogs.

CHEMISTRY

This is the top of the heap of the Science professions. You get to take matter apart, then put it back together again to see what you've got. What a thrill!

If you're a chemist you do tend to exude an odor of sulfur and rotten eggs, but your olfactory nerves will burn out so quickly you'll barely notice. Just ignore the wrinkled noses of disapproving laypersons. What do they know? They're not chemists. You are. And you're proud of it.

Tools of the Trade

Table of elements, Bunsen burner, lab table, crisp white smock.

HIGH-POWERED EXECUTIVE

This is the job of jobs, really; the mother of jobs, as Saddam Hussein might put it. Saddam Hussein might have made a good high-powered executive if he'd been given an army of ulcer-ridden lawyers instead of slavish colonels, armed with deal memos rather than loaded weapons.

High-powered executives have their offices on the top floors of the highest buildings in the cities where their companies are headquartered. Their companies always have mysterious names like Cyspex or Systyne, and their offices have nothing in them but a mahogany conference table the size of a landing field and one chair. The executives sit in the chair as corporate employees stand uncomfortably around the table. The HPEs review their holdings, bark a few commands, and then they're off on the helicopter to the private jet, which will whisk them away to another city.

Tools of the Trade

Private jet, helicopter, Italian suits, underlings.

MAVERICK EXECUTIVE

A leaner version of the high-powered executive, mavericks require no office. All they need is an exotic assistant (Belgians or Jamaicans are preferred) to hand them papers, the cellular phone, or the laptop computer at a previously arranged signal. Mavericks spend their days purchasing corporations, gutting each successive corporation to raise money to pay for the last purchase. The maverick is the corporate equivalent of a homeless person.

Tools of the Trade

Exotic assistant.

MATHEMATICS

Not much of a profession, unless your idea of a good job is to run around mumbling unsolvable equations to yourself. However, elements of math do come in handy at tax time, such as figuring out how much you owe your accountant. Also, math plays a major role in shopping, bookkeeping, and calculus, three things essential to any profession.

Tools of the Trade

Chalkboard, chalk, calculator, aspirin.

NUMISMATICS

The study of coins. This is not a profession in itself, but if you opt for, say, a career in banking, knowing the difference between a dime and a quarter can give you a competitive edge.

Tools of the Trade

One of those big books bound in Leatherette which, when opened, reveals a number of semicircular slots, each of which is meant to hold a coin. If you're a selfish person who likes to hoard (and who isn't?), numismatics may be a career to consider.

PHYSICS

Subatomic physics is quite the rage with young people today, but my hunch is it's just a short-lived fad. Become a subatomic physicist and, mark my words, you'll be left with nothing to show for your life but a handful of theoretical particles. That and a dime won't even get you a cup of coffee. Believe me, I've been there.

Tools of the Trade

Linear accelerator.

PSYCHOLOGY

This is the study of the mind. It comes in handy in the fields of market research, politics, and used-car sales. Taken by itself, psychology is introspective and passive, unlike action-oriented chemistry. It's always your choice, of course, but if you become a psychologist, there's probably something wrong with you.

Tools of the Trade

Two-way mirrors, Van Dyke beard, elbow patches, tweedy clothing, corduroy sports coats, thick Austrian accent, very nice couch, patients.

SECRETARY

Knowing you're the secret power behind any well-run office is a kick, but your boss will invariably turn out to be a fool, a boor, or both. Plus, you can't wear comfortable shoes at your desk, so you are forced to carry appropriate yet uncomfortable shoes to work in your purse or purselike accessory. Every morning you will see thousands of others like yourself, pouring from the pneumatic doors of public transportation, all smartly dressed, fresh, crisp, and clean except for the battered Reeboks on their feet. You are but one lonely person in a faceless crowd, united only by comfy shoes which cannot be worn on company time.

Much brooding along these lines can lead even the most efficient secretary into depression, and the desire to own a cat.

Tools of the Trade

Multiline phone, various databases, many shoes.

MISCELLANY

The manufacture of stainless steel or Velcro is always a sure bet. The field of medicine, while not strictly a Science (too service-oriented) will make your parents proud—a factor to consider at least in passing. If you're good with your hands, you could start a business at home making pith helmets. There will always be a market for pith. You could start a frog farm. Or go into desktop publishing and grab a slice of the market on self-help books, lab manuals, or tables of random numbers.

You could become an assistant to a Scientist. I have one, named Rodney. I don't pay him much. I don't pay him at all, in fact. But one day, when I am but selenium dust, all my knowledge will be his. As Robert Blake used to say, "You can take that to the bank."

SERVICE PROFESSIONS

Though none approach the clinical joy Science provides, there are other professions. These include those which serve others.

Once confined strictly to butlers, chauffeurs, and maids, the so-called service professions have blossomed under the past few presidents, providing jobs to tens of thousands and giving a real shot in the arm to Republican employment figures.

Service offers such exciting careers as fast-food cashier, express-lane bank teller, desk clerk, convenience-store night manager, or trance channeler.

But there's more to service, much more. Want to be a stockbroker? The stockbroker provides financial advice that will lose millions, for a nominal fee. Those nominal fees can really add up. Stressful and money-making, stockbroking is still a coming profession even in the nineties.

If you're incompetent and a swell dresser, you might try becoming a consultant. A consultant doesn't do anything really, but he or she does it in an office made entirely of anodized aluminum, an office which holds only a bulging Rolodex, and a briefcase so slim nothing can fit in it. I may go into consultancy myself, if this Science thing ever dries up.

ENTERTAINMENT

While not a public service in any sense of the word, the American entertainment industry does employ many otherwise unemployable people.

Take stars. Though stars have fragile egos and lack any marketable skill, somehow they are role models for youth everywhere. Without the entertainment industry, stars would be roaming the streets cadging money for cosmetic surgery. Instead they earn millions of dollars!

And they spread it around among an entire support industry.

There are producers, coaches, referees, directors, musicians, engineers, editors, writers. . . . In the film industry alone you can find employment as a gaffer, a best boy, or a grip. I don't know what these jobs are, but I do know they pay top dollar.

There's even a support industry for the support industry: publicists, agents, personal managers, lawyers, groupies, and talk show hosts. All you have to do is find your star and hang on for the ride.

MUSICIAN

Here's a good profession if you're a night person. The only drawback is you may have to change your name to Something-T, or Something-Ice, or stick with an even simpler name like Cher, Liberace, or Hildegarde.

Most musicians are deficient in the IQ department, their brains being hardwired to emphasize other, noncognitive abilities. Consequently, your average musician cannot remember his last name, and the one-name system was developed to help these unfortunates. Often musicians will wear something akin to a dog tag which gives his or her full name, Social Security number, current address, phone number, and some rudimentary instructions, like "Please make sure I get home! Reward!"

This never works, however. No self-respecting person would claim a reward for the simple act of helping a musician offstage and home. Would you charge a lost child for finding his parents? There is hope that musicians can be taught some simple tricks to help them remember more than one word at a time. Singer k.d. lang, for example, has added two initials to her name, at the expense of capitalization. This may be a first step on the long road to complete polysyllabicism for all musicians, except drummers, of course.

CROONERS AND VERTEBRATE PALEONTOLOGISTS

Alas, I fear Harry Connick, Jr., may have killed off the crooner profession forever. There is hope for vertebrate paleontologists however, if we keep children interested in dinosaurs. I don't know if vertebrate paleontologists like to think of themselves as providing fantasy material for four-year-olds, but that's the truth of it.

CIVIL SERVICE

Running for public office might be chancey, but there are plenty of other civil service jobs that can provide a lifetime of pleasure.

A bureaucrat, for example, can wallow in the red tape the rest of us merely wade through. You can join a grant committee and shell out thousands of tax dollars to underfed performance artists. You can become a policeman, teacher, or any number of underpaid and despised professions that go a long way toward paying the rent, if your spouse and children also work.

Mail delivery is the profession to go for in this category. Contrary to popular belief, the post office really does collect all the mail at all the boxes at 5:00 P.M., just like it says on the box. What they don't tell you is what they do with the mail after they pick it up. Often they take it to a warehouse and let it sit there for days. Sometimes, just for fun, they take it to another mailbox and let it wait there until 5:00 P.M. the next day. You see, mail persons are human too, and they get tired of the day-in-and-day-out routine; picking up, sorting, and delivering the mail finally gets to them. So they try to make it zany, unpredictable, and fun.

Mail persons get to carry huge leather pouches and wear pith helmets. Plus, they're outdoors all day. Beats banging on a typewriter for eight hours under fluorescent lights.

CRIME

If you like looking for loopholes, you'd probably make an excellent lawyer. On the flip side of that coin, drug dealers and professional killers also make a very good living. And they don't report their earnings to the IRS! Life is a lot cheaper than it used to be, but if you're not averse to murder in quantity, you could probably goose your income to preinflationary levels.

BLUE-COLLAR

I'd pass on this field. All blue-collar workers are rapidly being replaced by robots.

PHARAOH

Embarking on this career involves the use of a trance channeler, who will demand ten percent or more of your wealth, but you'd still be left with plenty—scores of Nubian slaves, sensual and sinister priests of Isis, ankhs, and gold-encrusted scarabs. The icing on the cake? You get to send mummies into the future to kill archaeologists! It's an exotic profession, sure, but being a Pharaoh is nothing to be sneezed at.

REALTOR

See Appendix: The Real Realtor.

SUCKERS, SAPS, MARKS

One measure of how far we've fallen is the length of time it takes to make a sucker these days. Was it a mere century ago that one was born every minute? Nowadays it takes only thirty seconds to create a fully formed sucker. Of course the quality of workmanship is much lower, now that everyone wants easy big money with little or no effort behind it. And the new suckers just don't suck as hard as the ones made a few years back. It's probably just another indicator of the death of our species—we're too lazy even to feed anymore. If we're not spoon-fed a diet of spice cake and wine, we'd just as soon starve. I say leave the sucking to those who really want the job. Too many chiefs, not enough Indians, if you know what I mean.

TO DO AND SEE

To see if you're even in the ballpark when it comes to understanding the true ramifications of the home and its many parts, take the following multiple-choice test. One wrong answer means you should probably rent rather than own. Two wrong answers tells you you'd do well to buy a service agreement with any appliance purchase. Three wrong answers and you should live in hotels, carrying only what you can fit in a couple of suitcases.

1. Television runs on water, except when the program is really hot, and then it runs on: (a) steam. (b) phlogiston. (c) phlegm. (d) hydrogen.
2. Your typical vacuum cleaner bag is an amoebic life form that needs to be changed every: (a) ten minutes. (b) never. (c) time you use it. (d) time you think an impure thought.
3. Abraham Lincoln invented the rotary phone. Who was the first person he called? (a) Edgar Cayce (b) John Wilkes Booth (c) Howard Cosell (d) Ann-Margret
4. Everyone with two brain cells that connect knows that matter can neither be created nor destroyed. What effect does this have on

God? (a) None. God does not exist. (b) God is really, really mad about it. (c) The instant someone figured this out, God ceased to exist. (d) Satan is behind all scientific endeavor, so this realization made him happy.

5. If you were stuck on a raft in the middle of the ocean with a lump of coal, a can of shoe polish, and Uncle Joe from *Petticoat Junction*, what is the first thing you would do? (a) Ask Uncle Joe to tell you what Bobbie Jo and Betty Jo are really like. (b) Throw Uncle Joe overboard, blacken your face with shoe polish, and eat the lump of coal. (c) Eat the shoe polish, throw yourself overboard, and forget about the lump of coal. (d) I can't remember what the question was.

Now that you've passed this test, you're ready to move on to the mysterious innards of the house itself. It would be easy to quit now, pat yourself on the back for having tried something a bit difficult, and go back to that novel you bought at the airport magazine stand.

But instead, just for the heck of it, let's be brutally honest with ourselves. Don't you really want to learn more? Don't you want to become the Master of yourself and your environment? Turn the page.

FAMOUS HOMES

1. MONTICELLO

   Thomas Jefferson was still working on it, and the house remained unfinished at the time of his death.

2. THE WHITE HOUSE

   Even Franklin Roosevelt was a mere tenant. One *occupies* the White House, one doesn't *live* there.

3. THE PALACE AT VERSAILLES
   Sure, it was a great place to live, if you didn't mind ending up with your head on a chopping block.
4. HOME ON THE RANGE
   Freedom of movement has its price: snakes, scorpions, bad coffee, and cattle stampedes.
5. COTTAGE BY THE SEA
   Talk to me about your damp little love nest in ten years. We'll see how perfect it seems then.
6. SOD HUT
   This is the house that built the West, but they were torn down as soon as their occupants could afford lumber, now weren't they?
7. XANADU ("KUBLA KHAN")
   Beyond inspiring an unfinished poem by Samuel Coleridge, what is its true comfort value?
8. XANADU (*Citizen Kane*)
   Beyond inspiring a flawed movie by Orson Welles, what is its true comfort value?
9. RANCH-STYLE HOME
   The word *style* betrays the central flaw in the concept. What is a ranch without cattle? And who would tolerate cattle in the suburbs?
10. DINGY FLAT OR APARTMENT
    Only an artist can survive in a dingy flat, and artists, as we know, are subsidized at the taxpayer's expense. How can a bad poet (or performance artist) ever find personal bliss knowing that it can only be achieved at federal expense?

4

YOUR HOME AND YOU

In a very real sense, we are our homes.

This statement may seem extreme. The reader is tempted to respond, ''What Dr. Science meant to say is that our homes are an expression of us.'' No, gentle reader, I chose my words carefully. We are our homes, and our homes are us. This is the mystical union of housing and personhood, which is as intricately interspersed as marshmallows in lime Jell-O, though Science does not yet know which is which.

The first thing we must do if we are to appreciate our homes is to identify with them. That door is a bit off square, and isn't our one toenail a bit askew as well? There are bald spots on the lawn and our scalps. The basement is damp and we could stand a change of socks. It does us no good to pull the animate-versus-inanimate trip on our house. Our house could care less what elitist attitudes we bring to it.

We are the ones struggling for a sense of security, of being at home. Where can we relax and feel we truly belong, if not at home? But how can we relax and feel among friends if our house and its many appliances, pipes, wires, ducts, studs, and panels are foreign to us?

We can't, and the money we might throw away on psychiatry could better be spent on home improvement. So let's dig in, shall we? Let's get intimate with our homes, before we're too alienated to live anywhere at all.

LOCATION, LOCATION, LOCATION

When asked where they live, people from small towns often say they live in the middle of nowhere. Yet you will find that most people who say they live in the middle of nowhere are unacquainted with each other. This is easily explained.

The fourth dimension has the unique property of being everywhere and nowhere at once. Now, when this fourth dimension, the so-called space/time continuum, is ripped, ozone leaks out to repair the hole. So if you detect the telltale scent of hypertriplicated oxygen, it's surefire proof that you are indeed in the middle of nowhere. If you don't smell ozone, then you're probably somewhere else entirely, unless you hear the theme from *The Twilight Zone* being played faintly in the background. In either case, you probably are where you think you are.

Many large cities, on the other hand, are often described as being anywhere and nowhere, as having "no *there* there." The urban environment is being steadily obscured by neon, indifference, and grime.

It's also being slowly effaced by suburban resentment, as suburbia, where most of us now live, strives to achieve the status of Anywhere, USA. But if suburban reality is less that of a Steven Spielberg movie than *A Nightmare on Elm Street*, it is not alone.

As the infrastructure crumbles, pundits speak of the forgotten middle class, the silent majority, disenfranchised youth, undertaxed rich, and so forth. This sense of alienation and lack of self-esteem that pervades the modern dwelling can only be blamed on what the third-rate Frenchman, Jean-Paul Sartre, called "other people."

LIVING WITH OTHERS: A CAUTIONARY NOTE

The most meaningful relationships are built on dishonesty. For a relationship to work well, it must first be based on a highly select group of facts and assumptions. These are carefully edited from a much larger group of facts and assumptions, sometimes referred to by philosophers as Truth.

Just as a person with a receding chin prefers to hide that area beneath a luxurious beard, so do potential lovers and friends mask their darker natures beneath sunny effervescence and false cheer.

Who besides a Satanist wants to become intimate with someone else's demons? Not even a therapist wishes to wrestle with that aspect of the subconscious Freud called the *Verschrechtermann*, or Fat Man Who Smells Bad.

Marriage counselors confirm this fact. Ninety-nine percent of those who stay married more than a decade survive because they indulge only in pleasant banter and avoid all but the most cursory contact. Duration of marriage is inversely proportional to depth of interaction.

This is not to suggest there is no hope for marriage, or any other extended working or personal relationship. Rather that only by reducing our inflated expectations of honesty and candor can we hope to rid our lives of constant disappointment and frustration. Only when we gird ourselves with the weapons of skepticism and casual disinterest will we find ourselves able to meet the world on its own terms. A well-armed citizenry is the bulwark of democracy!

But how does mistrust happen? When do human beings deny the rights of equality and compassion to their fellow humans? The answer is simple: when they become neighbors.

BRASS TACKS

These are the faces of your neighbors.

BOB

Whether in the guise of playboy or family man, Bob is the prime breeder of resentment among home-dwellers.

The playboy's sports car squeals to a halt at midnight, crammed to its sidewalls with vibrant supermodels. As they spill into his sleek love shack, their squeals of delight keep you from sleep. Husband and wife roam the darkened halls of their mortgaged home, toting up bills in their heads, as the muted strains of the playboy's sensual jazz platters waft out over the heads of an insomnia-ridden neighborhood. Is this unrepentant pleasure-seeker among anxious working stiffs not a chastisement, a mockery?

Bob the executive, on the other hand, is too perfect. He occupies a highly paid position in his company, yet his children worship him and do well in school. His very attractive wife is devoted to his every need, yet finds time to be active in community affairs. Bob is fit, loving, friendly, and on a first-name basis with everybody in a three-block radius. On the rare nights when sleep comes to his less perfect neighbors, their dreams are full of longing—that some criminal will ding the fender of Bob's Mercedes, or plant crabgrass on his lawn, or that Bob's wife will be discovered in the playboy's arms, drunk in the driveway at some predawn hour.

BITTER RETIRED PERSONS

Every district has more than its share of the sullen elderly. They put in their forty years and what do they have to show for it? Their children hate them and they're trapped in a loveless marriage and a paid-off house they're sick of living in. During the day, they stand in their living rooms, glaring out their picture windows. At night, they shut themselves up with television programs that insult their intelligence, only amusing themselves by calling 911 every time a teenager drives by the house.

BROODING MEN IN FEED CAPS

If they have a job, they hate it. They also hate their children, their wives, and you. They have guns. Sometimes they take high-powered rifles into their yellowed back yards and fire wildly at the moon.

RECENT IMMIGRANTS

Doesn't their very eagerness, their happiness at being in America, make you want to throw obstacles in their path? Isn't their very hopefulness a reminder of your failed dreams?

JUST PLAIN JOES AND JANES

These are the people like you. Contrary to popular belief, the knowledge that there are others as miserable as you are does not lead to comfort. It only leads to a feeling of being trapped.

PHYSICIST

Why won't your neighbor give you the time of day? Before you get insulted, consider: Perhaps he's a physicist. As such, he may not even know what time of day it is. He'd be all too aware of the interchangeability of time and space. Even if he could tell you the time of day, then most certainly he wouldn't be able to tell you where you are. So it's a trade off. Not only is the poor slob laboring under Einstein's outmoded theory of relativity, he's also probably aware of Heisenberg's Uncertainty Principle. So give the guy the benefit of the doubt. Do him a favor and leave him alone.

LAWN CARE AND HOME SECURITY

Though joggers and dogs both share a fondness for other people's lawns (and for many of the same reasons), lawns are not created by their owners as a gesture of generosity for these or any other passers-by. This should be evident by now. Like most human endeavors, massive, compulsive lawn building is based on fear—fear of other people. A fearful foundation is a firm one, rooted in instinct that goes back to the dawn of time. A man's lawn is his moat, a grass barrier between one's home and one's neighbors. Choked with herbicides, pesticides, weeds, and a sprinkling of grass, it is a formidable obstacle to pedestrian traffic.

Even our sporting events are, in essence, a form of lawn worship. After all doesn't AstroTurf, the ersatz lawn of choice nowadays, separate the fans from their team, and the teams from each other? Fans clearly are there to become one with that vast lawn below. AstroTurf fills the need for grass in the collective unconscious, using petroleum products and minimal sustained human effort.

But how can all this explain the thrill a homeowner gets when first mowing his lawn? How can simple pheromones cause the endorphin rush that follows a whiff of newly mown grass? The ragged roar of a two-cycle engine, the sharp scent of gasoline, the green clots of grass disgorged from the side vent of the mower? These are the sensual signposts that tell us that summer is indeed ''icummen in.''

Likewise, a sad wilted quilt of brown grass allows us to appreciate our indoor wall-to-wall carpeting (much of which is made of the same chemical fibers found in AstroTurf!).

Thanks to Science and industry, our bare feet need never touch bare earth again. This comforting thought stays with us year round, unlike many so-called discoveries which are news items one day and public embarrassments the next.

YOUR GARDEN

Again, you have a garden not to enjoy its alleged fruits, but to contrast them to your neighbors'. A garden is both a celebration and parody of the agricultural impulse that led the human race from its tribal path of hunting/gathering to the stone-free road of agriculturalism. A garden is something to defend. This should be apparent. That being said, let me admit that I myself have a garden (hydroponic) and have some parenthetical tips.

WORMS

Next time you're digging in your garden, pick up a common angleworm and take a close look at it. You'll notice it doesn't have any eyes. How then, you might wonder, do they know where they're going?

The answer is simple: They don't. Worms know surprisingly little, considering how long they've been around. Are there worm Scientists, artists, composers of note? Of course not. Worms are the underachievers of the animal kingdom. Don't waste your time feeling sorry for worms; they deserve their miserable lot.

TULIPS

If you grow tulips you may notice that when bulbs sprout, some are yards away from where they were planted and where they flowered a year ago. If you happen to notice this phenomenon, listen to me. Get out of the house now. Don't turn back. Don't stop to gather your valuables. You've somehow gotten hold of the assassin tulip bulbs developed by the now-disbanded Dutch Secret Service (*Securitate*). These migrating tulips were bred to lie dormant for a season, then when the casual gardener least expects it, they move and sprout. The original nightstalking tulips were developed for use by NATO, but a clerical error listed them in the Burpee Seed Catalog. Thousands were mailed inadvertently, COD, to the States. Undoubtedly they've gotten into your house and are under your bed waiting to pierce your mattress and you in a night of blooming death. I repeat, though it's probably too late, get out of your house now.

OTHER PESTS

While we're on the subject, and before we go inside to explore further American domicidal tendencies, let us discuss and dismiss some common household pests.

SPIDERS AND COBS

One of the perils of housecleaning are those unsightly gray, flimsy, fibrous masses which accumulate in the corners near the ceiling. These are called cobwebs. When you find a spiderweb, a spider is usually close by, munching on a housefly, but one seldom sees a cob.

There's a reason for this. Cobs only spend a small amount of time indoors. The rest of the time they're in the fields, making corn silk. The time they do spend spinning webs they spend efficiently. While it takes a spider the better part of a day to spin a medium-sized web, a cob can lace an entire basement or attic ceiling in a matter of minutes. Cobs are easily bored, and often spin webs just to be doing something. The term *cobbler* comes from the cob, the most humble and industrious of the arachnids. Yes, spiders get all the publicity, but it's the lowly cobs who do all the dirty work.

ANTS

It's common knowledge that electrical outlets attract ants. This appears to be a process of self-mortification. Inspired by the discipline endured by the saints, these pious ants test the limits of their endurance for pain by walking straight into 120 volts AC. If you think an involuntary shock hurts you when you accidentally touch a frayed extension cord, imagine what it must feel like to a creature a thousand times smaller than you. Of course we must bear in mind that ants are also a thousand times stronger than we would be if we were their size, and they are nothing if not determined. Their quest for spiritual progress makes even the most pious human seem an unrepentant sinner.

MOTHS

If moths are so attracted to lights, you wonder, why don't they all fly into the sun?

Well, check your assumptions. The fact is, moths hate lights, and they're simply trying to destroy them. Sure it's a suicide mission, but that's how much they hate artificial lights. They hate the sun too, but not nearly as much. After artificial lighting, the next items on the moth hit list are oldies stations and self-help books. Moths attack both with a vengeance. They are largely indifferent to polyester clothing, but are fond of wool. They attack wool not out of fury, but passionate delight. Interfere in their relationship with wool, and you risk having a few thousand moths attack your eyes, which are the lamps of the soul.

TERMITES

These pesky antlike insects are not related to ants in any way. They are pseudoneuropterous social insects who can reduce any wooden house to sawdust in seconds. The only way to get rid of these creatures also known as the six-legged piranha, is to seal your entire house hermetically and pump in anteaters, which, confused by the darkness, will think the termites are ants and devour them. Your house will then be infested by anteaters, of course, but they are easily trained and can even prove useful in ridding your garden of aphids, tent caterpillars, and inchworms. They are not, however, affectionate. And even anteaters won't eat slugs.

SLUGS

Also not related to the ant in any way, this slow-moving, slimy gastropod, also known as the "living tongue," is extremely ugly.

That it even shares the planet with us makes one wonder at the value of existence at all.

WATERING

A backyard teeming with salamanders, humming with cicadas, and athrob with the muted domestic disputes of the neighbors would seem to be a place you would want to avoid.

But no! Some of us would spend every waking hour pruning, mulching, and muttering over tattered lettuce leaves if we could. Those of us who don't have a swimming pool, which necessitates ripping up every piece of green growth on the property and replacing it with tasteful aquamarine tiles, compensate for that loss by watering everything in sight.

When we're not watering our miserable, parched excuse for a lawn, its bare patches baked hard as concrete under an unmerciful sun, the rest crawling with kudzu or some other plant form spawned in hell, we're washing our cars—as if through recreating, however briefly, the gleaming machine we first saw on the showroom floor, without the dents, the mileage, and melted chocolate in the back seat, we can entertain the fantasy of escape, of letting slip the domicidal bonds and driving fast down a nameless freeway, radio on and the top down. Of course, if you don't own a convertible, this can be a disastrous daydream. Yes, when fantasy meets a garden hose, it can really raise havoc with a Leatherette interior.

PLUMBING: HOSES TO HEALTH

Our bodies are a veritable waterworks, pipes carrying precious fluids hither and yon. But what are you going to do if hither is flooded and yon is drying out? Are there plumbers for this sort of thing? Do they work nights?

Of course not. Your body is a temple. You are that temple's

high priest. It's up to you to keep your plumbing in shape. Yet how quickly we believe the opposite to be true when it comes to our homes!

The basement is flooded? The pipes are frozen? Let's call the plumber! Sure, let's bring in someone else to take care of something *we* should have been taking care of all along.

Your plumber has no respect for you. He knows that you're too lazy or incompetent to treat your home with enough TLC to make his visits unnecessary. And your house has no respect for you either. Because you have no respect for yourself.

An elementary law of Science states that *your home is an outward expression of your inward reality*. This rather clumsy sentence is the basis for the discipline known as architecture, which is actually an *applied* form of psychiatry.

Let's begin our careful exploration of the house's interior with the seat of dysfunction and of terror: the bathroom.

PERSONAL HYGIENE

A clean body is quite often an indicator of a diseased and septic mind. One who spends an inordinate amount of time washing, grooming, and perfuming his body doesn't have the time to spend the countless hours in the lab necessary to get real work done.

Consequently, if someone who looked like George Hamilton or Pat Boone called himself a Scientist it would be the worst kind of chicanery, a black crime that cries to heaven for justice!

I'm sure this Scientist is not alone in his vehement dislike of anyone who looks like George Hamilton, Pat Boone, or Tab Hunter breezing through life on his looks, and having the audacity to call himself a Scientist. Women throw themselves at a guy like that, and no wonder. He never smells of the sweat engendered by hard work, his hair is never rife with the salts of heavy metals or mildly radioactive isotopes, his fingernails are never stained with iodine or chromium.

No, a guy like that just drifts through life, dabbing on aftershave and checking his reflection in the rearview mirror of his fancy convertible.

Of course, there are certain operations that are cost- and time-effective when it comes to personal hygiene. These include rinsing the mouth with a solution of stannous fluoride diluted in hydrochloric acid; rubbing various emollients, suspended animal fats, and glycerated esters on the skin; and combing the hair with a comb or some other combing device.

But none of these behaviors will guarantee that one day you'll glide through life like George Hamilton, Pat Boone, Tab Hunter, or George Maharis, always having somebody else pick up the restaurant tab and a miniskirted supermodel on either arm as your chauffeur drives the bunch of you to the beach for another day of loafing and sex games.

Grooming and personal hygiene are of limited importance. Far more important are personal integrity and character, qualities that cannot be purchased in a tube or bottle, even if you are George Hamilton, Pat Boone, Tab Hunter, George Maharis, or Richard Chamberlain, none of whom, I might add, can act their way out of a paper bag.

THE SHOWER

Be that as it may, the shower is the center of the modern home. After a hard day at the office, or with the kids, or in the backyard torching kudzu, a hot shower sounds good, doesn't it?

Perhaps you've noticed that your heartbeat accelerates slightly when you get out of a hot shower. Why is this? Well, you're falling in love, generally with your soap or shampoo. You see, even though we step into hot water to get clean, we tend to be attracted to anyone or anything that sees us in the buff. This is only human.

If you'd rather that the object of your desire be something other than inanimate, I recommend exposing yourself to something higher up the evolutionary scale, something alive at least. This is why I firmly believe fungus and mold should be allowed to stay on your bathroom fixtures. Life is a constant struggle against loneliness; why let a compulsive urge for cleanliness interfere with your pathetic reaching out for comfort?

From fungus, you can gradually work yourself up to humans, if you can find one willing to bathe or shower with you in those moldy surroundings. Remember, if you do fall in love with one of your own, and it doesn't work out, you can always hit the showers.

Showers are notorious for being nonjudgmental. You get the same adjustable spray no matter what your personal beliefs are. Need proof? Well, Science knows that only your toes and fingers are wrinklable. The rest of you is already wrinkled to capacity. Your shower also knows this about you. That's why only your fingers and toes get what Science calls "wrinkly" in the bathtub. The shower somehow knows that, like the Saggy Baggy Elephant, humans are a hideous composite of wrinkles, stretch marks, and sags. So it appeals to your desire for uniformity on a subconscious level.

Scientists are working on this problem, by the way, but so far Elasti-skin is only in the developmental stage. The prototypes keep ripping during even moderate exercise. Of course, Congress could sink large amounts of cash into the project and hurry things along, but we're so used to our grotesque selves that we think we have more pressing uses for our money.

Another user-friendly aspect to the shower is that you can create life in the bathtub, easy. Mix twelve dozen cartons of Jell-O in your bathtub, run 220 volts of electricity through it, and there you are. Science even has a hunch that this is probably how all life itself began, when the Supreme Scientist let His curiosity prod Him to zap a celestial bathtub full of Jell-O. Psychologists might waste their time and ours by wondering why anyone in his right mind would want to electrocute a gelatinous blob, but it is only by saying no to the rules and yes to the impulse that real beginnings are made.

But there's another more sinister side to the shower. Many times after a shower you may notice clumps of hair clogging the drain. Before you rush to your local pharmacist in a panic, trying to stock up on Minoxidyl, consider this: It may not be your hair at all. It may be the shower's hair. It may not be going down the drain; it may be coming up!

Of course this is just an hypothesis, but my personal theory is that when this hair or hairlike substance sees you staring at it, it pretends to flow back down the drain. You see, your shower may want to kill you. All this lovey-dovey stuff with voyeurism and the wrinkles may be just a screen for its murderous intentions. Just to be on the safe side, I recommend that you never take long showers. Anything over five minutes could give that hair the time it needs to reach your ankles. From there it would be a simple job to pull your feet out from under you. The old saw has it that many accidents happen in bathtubs. I happen to think they weren't accidents at all.

So there you have it. The shower is a mixed bag of creativity and destruction, a paradigm of the modern home. Unwilling to cope with the shower's contradictory nature, I myself no longer use it.

Water hasn't touched my skin since the summer of '65. That's when I discovered that a daily sponge bath with a few cc's of isobutanol does a better job of personal hygiene than three hundred gallons of soapy aitch-two-oh. Why do you still shower? Like the shower, I make no judgment. We are all prodded into action by great unconscious forces moving just beneath the surface of our minds. It would be naïve of you to think you're immune to such compulsion. Any attempt at making a natural law out of a personal habit is at best arrogance, and at worse ignorance. That said, let's move on.

THE CABINET

Here again, we find denial rearing its ugly head. I challenge America to examine its own bathroom. Throw open your medicine cabinet! What do you see? Half-used packets of dental floss, tiny bottles of shampoo from cheap hotels, once-used disposable razor blades, half-squeezed tubes of salty toothpaste you purchased at a health-food store in a fit of eco-mania, useless headache remedies, and iffy birth control devices. Liberate yourself! Throw it all away, and acknowledge the emptiness of your life. And absorb these facts:

Q-TIPS

The Q in Q-Tip stands for Quetzalcoatl, the winged serpent-god of Aztec legend. Aztecs used tiny poison darts with cotton wadding on one end, which were shot from blow pipes. During the festivals of Quetzalcoatl, happy celebrants would shoot each other with these darts, stopped with cotton on both ends. When an enterprising Aztec pharmacist took a dart in the ear, he found how effective they were for hygiene. Thus the Quetzalcoatl tip was born. Queztalcoatl tips were popular all over Mexico until the Spanish arrived. Unable to pronounce it, they shortened the name to Q-Tips. So the Aztecs may be gone, but their art, architecture, and the Q-Tip are eternal reminders of their greatness.

BELLY BUTTON LINT

Belly button lint always matches the color of the T-shirt worn by the bearer of the lint at the time of its discovery. That's a natural law. If one were interested in sartorial splendor, one could find an outfit that would make a lint that would be the envy of a rainbow. Here we see our insane obsessiveness with personal appearance, paradoxically, interfering with our ability to make a fashion statement.

ASPIRIN BOTTLES

The cotton inside an aspirin bottle isn't cotton at all, but the aspirin's nest. It is made when a bottle of aspirin sits on the store shelf too long; the aspirin inside reaches maturity and begins to breed. When you casually toss the bottle into the wastebasket, you also tear open their little love nest. This is just one reason why aspirin hate us. You've probably discovered by now that aspirin does little to relieve your aches and pains, and you've graduated to ibuprofen, which doesn't hate us—yet. Mess with ibuprofen nests and you'll learn just how painful a headache can be.

TOOTH FAIRY

Science has determined that there is, in fact, a tooth fairy. (See Household Gods in the Appendix.) Its home away from home is your medicine cabinet. Ironically, however, the tooth fairy practices poor dental hygiene. It never brushes or flosses, though it will occasionally use mouthwash if its breath threatens to offend. Many members of the fairy genus gorge on candy just before bedtime. Health insurance is nonexistent in the fairy kingdom so the little people have to get inventive to meet their health needs. Elves often help themselves to medicines and hair products from your bathroom. If you find your shampoo isn't lasting as long as it used to, chances are good you have an elf infestation.

THE KITCHEN

A boon to the homemaker is a boon to us all. Where the kitchen used to be a place of drudgery, now it is a palace of pushbutton convenience. Today the lady of the house has leisure aplenty thanks to the many appliances Scientific Progress has given her. And if you believe all that, I'm a bridge in Brooklyn.

Let's learn more about these appliances, shall we?

THE REFRIGERATOR

Sometimes known as the icebox or Frigidaire, the refrigerator is home to countless foods and foodlike substances.

Contrary to popular belief, the refrigerator does not make things cold. It reinforces the coldness already present in things. This principle has been known since ancient times. Indeed, the first refrigerator, or "cold amplification box," was developed in 450 B.C. by Assyrian nomads looking to get out of the hunter/gatherer mode.

This box drew out the inherent coldness in objects by manipulating the subtle balances between vinegar and baking soda that exist in all matter. Heat, being more effusive than cold, is attracted to vinegar for the same reasons baking soda is. It's no coincidence that baking soda bears a strong resemblance to snow. Nor that nowadays, cartons of baking soda are placed in more than seventy percent of all refrigerators.

Is this novel use for a baking product merely the result of clever marketing strategy? Yes and no.

You ought to have your head examined if you believe that business about baking soda removing odors. Since when are refrigerator odors a problem? And what research has shown that baking soda does anything to absorb odors? No, it's all a lie, and a whopper at that.

But was it the simple desire to misinform that prompted baking soda manufacturers to fabricate such a tale? Not totally. It has at least as much to do with their desire to keep refrigerators operating efficiently until the warranty expires. The half-life for cold-amplification potential in a single box of baking soda is five years. The standard refrigerator warranty? Five years. Coincidence? I doubt it.

THE FREEZER

Hard as it is to believe, there's a light that goes on inside your freezer as well, but unlike the light in the refrigerator, it's too cold to see it. Light slows down as it gets colder, stopping altogether at the freezing point, leading to a condition Science calls darkness. The converse is also true. The hotter it is, the faster light goes. This is why it's so hot on bright sunny days.

You can see the freezer light if you wish. Simply unplug your freezer and wait three hours. The time may be usefully passed by rereading *Principia Mathematica* by Sir Isaac Newton. Then put on your sunglasses and open your freezer. You will be deluged by a torrent of melted ice and your TV dinners will be a mess of soggy cardboard and tepid cranberry sauce, but the freezer's interior will be as bright as a new penny. Don't take my word for it. Observe on your own.

THE OVEN

The oven is a constant reminder of the chaos that rules the universe. ''Burn it down!'' is its silent cry. Both we and our homes would go down in flames if we let the oven have its way.

The self-cleaning oven is an antechamber to hell itself. Just as the hot-water heater is a cylindrical representation of aquatic Hades, so is the small hot room of your oven a taste of a possible afterlife, should you continue on your present course.

Since this Scientist would rather not dwell on the inevitable and unpleasant, I partake of food in its raw and temperate state.

THE MICROWAVE

Home microwaves are actually an extension of the home stereo. Microwaves themselves were developed during World War II as an antidote for nuclear radiation. The microwave ovens were a peacetime application for this new type of radiation. Originally developed as a unit to soften 78 rpm records, the microwave oven uses tiny, extremely energetic waves. These are called microwaves from the Greek *micro*, or dangerous, and *waves*, which translates here for our purposes as angry.

Why are these waves so angry? An outcast from the home entertainment center, failed buddy of our friend the atom, the microwave oven knows deep down it isn't welcome in our lives. Microwave ovens have no real function in the home, other than to take up counter space and overheat the insides of certain gooey food byproducts, which are then extremely effective at burning the inside of your mouth, even as the outside temperature of the product seems safe.

Nowadays there are many more effective ways to soften records when they become too brittle. Besides, most people today own CDs, which render record-softening outmoded. After all, only a fool would put a compact disc in a microwave oven. Likewise, there are easier, more satisfying ways to cook food and burn the inside of your mouth. So the microwave's effectivity is extremely limited. Yet the microwave, like a faithful mutt deliberately abandoned in the country, always seems to find its way home. Go figure.

THE TOASTER

Eldest of the appliance family, the toaster has freed us from the dangerous and painful practice of holding bread slices into an open flame. In those olden days, toast-making could often prove fatal.

But do we thank our lucky stars for toasters? Of course not. Not in my book. The toaster seems deceptively simple, but let's take a closer look at the toaster's strange work behind the scenes.

You place the bread into the toaster's slots. Then you press a little sliding thingamajig down. A few moments later your bread pops back up, toasted. Or does it?

Appearances can be deceiving.

Close molecular analysis has shown that the toasted bread you get back is not the same bread you placed in the slot. Toast is not twice-cooked bread. It's something else entirely.

Beneath your toaster, geologists now agree, there's a pneumatic conduit that leads straight to the center of the earth. There the slices of bread fed into your toaster feed thousands of hungry subterranean humanoids. No one knows for sure where these primitive mammals came from. Some believe they are the ancestors of space aliens who entered the center of the earth through the hole at the North Pole centuries ago. Some say these creatures have always lived there. Some even believe they are disgruntled former Rosicrucians who moved to the earth's core just before the Korean War. This is doubtful.

However they located in themselves in the bowels of the earth, they've found, much to their chagrin, that it's no garden spot. It's dark, hot, and stuffy as all get out. You can't grow food or raise livestock.

What was down there were huge chromium deposits. Fortunately for the subterraneans, they seemed to possess great manufacturing and marketing skills, as well as a love for toast. So they made bread-retrieval devices which they sold to the rest of us upstairs.

So they get our bread. What exactly do we get?

It seems that what we call toast is actually a specimen of Shingle Fungus, a nearly inedible scale that grows on the spherical walls of the earth's interior. It is entirely possible that earthquakes are actually the laughter of the core people at their practical joke. Some even theorize that these creatures have emerged in recent years, to work for H. Ross Perot. If so, perhaps the joke is on them.

THE COFFEEMAKER

The modern coffeemaker owes its existence to the great Joe DiMaggio. Joltin' Joe found that his game was greatly improved after he consumed multiple cups of espresso. But he also found that sitting in cafés in his native North Beach was time-consuming and expensive.

"There must be a better way," Joe thought to himself. "Someday I'm going to marry Marilyn Monroe and invent a way to make a good cup of coffee at home."

Although the two ideas were not connected, Joe pursued them with the same vigor he used to swing a baseball bat. In no time at all he came up with the first Mr. Coffee machine. When he showed his invention to his teammates Proctor Silex and Henry Mellita, they were skeptical. Both doubted that the public would be interested in eschewing the café scene to make coffee at home. But they were wrong, which is probably why they were into baseball and not retail.

Eventually, Joe's good friend Philo Farnsworth (the real inventor of television) suggested the modifications to the coffeemaker that assured its place on kitchen counters everywhere.

With Joe's prototype, you had to dip the whole coffeemaker into the sink in order to get water into it. Farnsworth suggested that there be a little grill on top through which one poured water. A simple enough idea, but one that had escaped Joe's fertile imagination.

Liberal ingestion of caffeine gave Joe many other ideas, but none caught on the way Mr. Coffee did. DiMaggio's rocket guidance system was briefly adopted by the Czechoslovakian Air Force, but abandoned due to its complexity.

THE BLENDER

In the Bob-the-playboy days of early marriage, it was a blender full of margaritas every night. You would tear each other's clothes away with your teeth, and swap tequila-tinged kisses right there on the spotless linoleum. Now, the linoleum is stained in the Bob-the-responsible-executive latter days of marriage, and the blender is only used to make chocolate shakes for your selfish young, the fruit of a useless, youthful passion.

THE JUICER

Like the baking soda toothpaste upstairs in the medicine cabinet and the Dr. Brown's tonic, the juicer gathers dust in an obscure corner. Bought on impulse after viewing a lively infomercial on cable television, it has done little more than enhance your credit rating and decrease your sense of self-worth.

THE DISHWASHER

Again, cascades of water are unleashed on inanimate objects to cleanse them of perceived imperfections. Once upon a time, we even used to scour these objects by hand!

And what are these objects? Two quart-sized cups from different convenience store giveaways, one emblazoned with the name of a professional football team, the other embossed with the cartoon likeness of a well-known movie star; the three forks, two knives, and one bent spoon that remain from the wedding collection, and the other silverware accumulated over the years; seven plates from seven different sets, the rest having been shattered or lost, the tiny shards missed by the broom embedded invisibly in floors all over the house; the big coffee mug that announces Dad, the delicate cup with pink roses around its rim; the Teflon pot that no longer bears a trace of Teflon; a blunt and rusted Ginsu knife; the big black iron pan that's the solid reminder of a country that used to make things to last. Ghosts, that's what you're washing, and every time you pour in the Joy it must be with a tinge of regret.

This is why I only eat from disposable foodware (which I toss into the eco-friendly linear accelerator), or with my bare hands.

FOOD GROUPS

While we're in the kitchen, we might as well get the subject of nutrition out of the way once and for all. What are the basic food groups? They are:

- *Coffee*
- *Fruits and Vegetables*
- *Carbohydrates*
- *Proteins*
- *Grease*
- *Popcorn*
- *Nachos*
- *Manna*
- *Pizza*

A balanced diet requires eating equal portions of each food group at least once a year. For instance, a breakfast of coffee and fish followed by a lunch of pizza and cheesecake would leave you wanting only a basket of walnuts for dinner. It's conceivable that you might not even want dinner, but be content with a liter or so of strong coffee before you retire for the evening.

All disease comes from an imbalance of these essential foods, aggravated by the desperate need for attention and general self-centered negativity fostered by a decaying society.

But don't fret. Despite what your mother told you, instead of eating these foods, you can indeed merely play with them. This is healing at its finest! In doing so, you can temporarily forget your inherent loneliness. Food that is toyed with is no longer referred to as "food," however, but as "pet."

COFFEE

The time has come to examine fully the pungent Bean Full O' Excitement. Let us begin with the following set of Coffee Realities:

1. You can never brew coffee too strong.
2. You can never drink too much coffee.
3. Coffee does not make you nervous. Your own inadequacies make you nervous. Coffee merely increases your perceptions of your own inadequacies.
4. The simplest way to drink coffee is orally, although injecting it intramuscularly or intravenously, dripping it directly into the eye, or bathing in it are also excellent ways to benefit from caffeine and its related alkaloids.
5. Tea is to coffee as ginger ale is to scotch.

Coffee is the first of the food groups that make up a balanced diet. It is the only food in these groups that can increase IQ and create energy without draining it in another area. "Sure," I hear you demur, "when I feel sleepy during the day, I drink coffee. But why is it, after a day of this I find myself awake when I want to go to sleep?" Because you're not drinking enough coffee!

Coffee is what makes America great! Sure, other nations have coffee, but nobody abuses it the way we do. Try to find a bottomless cup in a European restaurant. They make a big deal out of every refill. I've spent time in Latin America, but nobody ever offered to "warm that up for me," the way they do at your average American pancake house. We're a nation that can't sit still. We're in constant need of stimulation. We're jumpy. Irritable. And powerful. We have coffee to thank for the strong dollar, our balance-of-trade deficit, and an alert populace. Yes, thanks to coffee, we're Number One!

FRUITS AND VEGETABLES

This may shock you, but there is no difference, other than packaging, between fruits and vegetables. Vegetables are simply dried-out fruits, with most of the juice evaporated through the skin and the sweetness gone sour. There are other less essential differences, like the fact that fruits attract bugs at a far greater rate than vegetables, and the curious lack of consumer interest in vegetable-flavored chewing gum. I understand in certain countries they put sliced radishes on their cornflakes, but I've never visited such a place, and I doubt I ever will.

Here are some plant foods, however, you may wish to avoid.

Baby Corn

Baby corn is exactly what the name says, and it's a source of growing controversy. In Iowa, corn is planted every May, and by early July the baby corn is just clinging to the stalks. That's when farm workers armed with an implement resembling toenail clippers run through the rows, savagely clipping off the baby ears. This was a practice carried out in secrecy, until activists found out about it. Today protesters assemble in Iowa every summer to throw themselves in front of the cornstalks, occasionally even chaining themselves to the fledgling ears. These encounters between the so-called Corn Killers and Corn Peace Workers have received major attention in the Iowa news media, but not apparently in the rest of the nation. If you care, you can write to Corn Peace in Des Moines, Iowa, or you can just show up in the fields in July with your toe clippers and have a go at them. The choice is yours.

Fruitcake

The very existence of fruitcake is one of life's major unsolved mysteries. But now Science has provided some clues. The fruit in the fruitcakes is, of course, not really fruit at all. It comes from the frutite mines of Pueblo, Colorado, which were discovered in the late 1840s by seekers after gold. Though disappointed, these miners looked to find a use for this fruitlike, nearly edible mineral. So fruitcake was invented.

As we now know, frutite never degrades. Since the fruitcakes themselves are passed from giver to giver each Christmas and never eaten, the need for new fruitcake has long since ceased. The current problem is of disposal. There are plans to use an abandoned salt mine near Provo, Utah. Until this is filled, we'll be able to say at last not only where fruitcake comes from, but where it goes.

Raddicchio

This is the Antichrist of lettuce, and you risk eternal damnation if you eat it.

CARBOHYDRATES

Contrary to popular belief there are not twelve, but 459 ways that Wonder Bread builds strong bodies. The public relations department decided that people couldn't handle such a large number, so they reduced it to twelve. Of course there are many precedents for that number—the twelve apostles, the twelve steps of recovery, the twelve reasons to go on living (see Appendix).

Most of the methods have to do with intense carbo-loading, which is the physiological equivalent of using high-octane gasoline in your car. Horsepower is increased, but higher operating temperatures tend to burn out your exhaust system. When it comes to food, I stick to daily vitamin injections and a liter of distilled water.

PROTEINS

Fish

Fishing is murder. Most people don't want to face up to the fact that fish are nearly human. Many tuna can count up to a hundred in laboratory situations, and there are some flounder who can rebuild a carburetor. The trouble is, nobody wants to hear this, certainly not the sportsman, the consumer, or the food industry.

Fish Sticks

Before the McNugget there was the fish stick. Before being dumped in the deep-fat fryer, sticks were newly emerging organs on the ever-evolving fish. On the other hand, before fish sticks and chicken nuggets, both fowl and fish were of limited nutritional value. When these creatures spontaneously erupted in new, tastier body parts, better living through chemistry became a reality.

Of course it wasn't *really* a spontaneous development, it was the result of a lot of hard work by a large number of stern men in white lab smocks. As each one held a beaker full of brightly colored fluid to the light, each wondered, "Will this elixir hold the key to the lock that guards the clue to solve the mystery of what will make chicken or fish part of tomorrow?" Most chemists did very poorly at English composition, but you get the idea.

Hot Dogs

As you know, the government funding of space exploration allowed many marvels to enter the private sector which we would not otherwise possess. Personal computers and chrome-plated afterburners are perhaps the most dramatic of these innovations, but what about the thermostabilized hot dogs so popular with space shuttle crews? Where did they come from?

Thermostabilization itself was invented by Georg Gutenjahr, the man who discovered the vulcanization of rubber. A compulsive overeater, Gutenjahr was wolfing down a foot-long hot dog one day, while stirring a boiling pot of liquid latex. The hot dog fell into the pot, and when Gutenjahr retrieved it, he noticed that it was not only chewier, but foul-smelling and nearly inedible.

Well, one thing led to another, and soon thermostabilized hot dogs were on grocery store shelves everywhere. Since these hot dogs tasted much worse than their precursors, they were heavily advertised. Today the public can't buy them fast enough!

Spam

Spam grows from a spore. How did the spore get inside the can? It's the result of parthenogenic exulgism, a process involving bad smells, ill will, poor posture, and negative vibrations from a doomed military-industrial complex. I happen to enjoy Spam, as millions do. But that doesn't deny the fact that this product has a checkered past and an unsightly present. Still, it holds great charms for millions of consumers. As a matter of fact, just thinking about it makes me hungry.

Turkey Tetrazzini

I am well aware that a sizable number of my readers are avid lovers of both Italian food and tetravalent compounds made from birds. You might think that Turkey Tetrazzini would be just the ticket. Unfortunately, the last time I checked, Turkey Tetrazzini was nothing more than a decorative floor tile made by Du Pont. The so-called holiday themes in interior design started back in the 1950s when the general populace began to confuse wisdom with whimsy. True

Scientific progress doesn't mean making building supplies in the shapes of swine or fowl. A better tomorrow will be ours only if we keep our nose to the centrifuge and never let up! Remember what the Sputnik crisis felt like? Get to work, America!

Cheese Curls

Cheese curls, in fact, are the larval stage of a rare South American insect. At maturity, this worm is nine feet long and weighs close to half a ton. I never touch them. Neither should you.

Cheese Paper

No nutritive subtstitute has caught the imagination of the American public like cheese paper. This is the cheese that sticks to the wrapper of a fast-food cheeseburger, and is invariably tastier than the cheese on the burger itself! Amazing!

Developed in cooperation between the forest and chemical industries, cheese paper is manufactured in huge rolls of ten million double-ply sheets. Cheap, nutritious, delicious—cheese paper is why even if you forget today's hamburger, you won't forget the wrapping.

GREASE

Grease is the king of a superfood group all its own. Other members of this group include polysorbate 60, quaternium, mono- and diglyceride, and common gunk. All of the members of this food group are bad for you.

So why do we make them, and more important, why does a hungry public buy and consume them? Because they have the ability to cloud one's mind as well as one's arteries.

Grease is comparable to the likable guy who can't seem to hold down a job, pay his bills, or be trusted with money. You know he's trouble to be around but you can't bring yourself to tell him to get lost. Yes, the quality of mercy is not strained, as the Bard put it. Still, unstrained mercy is rare enough. Grease is the hair shirt of foods. We eat it to keep us humble.

POPCORN

We turn now to a burning question. Why do some popcorn kernels pop, and others just lie there?

Popcornologists have been pondering this question for years. At first they thought it was heredity, then environment, but since the percentage of non-poppers stays relatively constant regardless of ancestry or situation it is now commonly thought that some kernels simply lack the will to live. They are clinically depressed. No amount of coaxing, heating, or shaking the pan can stimulate these gloomy gus kernels to pop. So before you waste your money buying so-called gourmet popcorn at top dollar, first ask the salespeople if they're selling you happy, enthusiastic popcorn. If they don't know what you're talking about, buy your popcorn somewhere else.

MANNA

Manna from heaven is the perfect food. But it's also a celestial intrusion on the Fed's control of our money supply, and possession of such is now a federal offense.

NACHOS

Nacho dip is a yellow plasma found in arcades, dairy bars, and movie theaters. But more than that, it is nature's answer to manna. It is, in fact, the primordial slime from which all life sprang. This is why you should never put nacho dip in a microwave oven. The effects of the radiation could form an uncontrollable virus which could wipe out all life as we know it. Or you could get the dip too hot and burn the roof of your mouth. Either way, microwaves and nachos are a dangerous combination.

PIZZA

This handy disc comes in four Scientifically measured sizes: 6-inch, 8-inch, 10-inch, and 12-inch. It has the advantage of being the only food that contains all the major food groups. Many times, after skipping a few meals during a hard day at the lab, I'll take a slab of leavened bread, then slap on baby corn, Spam, popcorn, grease, and thinly sliced coffee beans. Put this in the oven at 350° for a half-hour, and you've got yourself a hearty meal that will keep you awake till dawn. I guarantee it.

FYI...

Every once in a while, when you open a box of cereal, you may notice a flake or oat ring outside the inner bag. Many people have written to ask me if these are safe to eat.

Sure—if your idea of a good time is having your stomach pumped. I'd rather take a hammer to my incisors than wolf down one of those topological refugees. There are malcontents in any system, and breakfast cereal is not immune from the sociological problems that affect the rest of creation. Nobody besides the manufacturer ever said that breakfast cereal is good for you. Eating noncomformist breakfast cereal is asking for trouble.

PETS

Many people own pets, in a misguided attempt to stave off loneliness. While I cannot condone pet ownership, I can understand and tolerate it. After all, I had sea monkeys when I was a kid. I also had a set of twelve highly trained planaria. When my mother inadvertently flushed them down the toilet, something broke inside me. This may be the source of my unreasonable hatred of biology. A therapist could probably answer that question, but unfortunately I have an unreasonable hatred of therapy as well. But I digress. Our issue is pets.

If a fish is lying poached on a plate, it is a meal. If it is swimming around in a tank, it is a pet. What's the difference between the two, beyond the obvious live-versus-dead thing?

The only difference is our attitude toward the fish. Yes, the only difference between a butcher shop and a pet shop is attitude. Many a turtle or salamander seems the same, dead or alive. Which is more annoying, a smelly, dead guinea pig or a squealing live one?

As I never tire of pointing out, a Yorkshire terrier makes a much more attractive throw rug than canine companion. A decade or so ago, someone came up with the idea of a pet rock. It wasn't really such a leap of imagination considering the average IQ of many pets and the desperate yearning of pet owners.

So a pet is any potential food product that has the capacity to distract us from our own unhappiness. In that way alcoholic beverages could be seen as a variety of pet, albeit a vicious, liquid one.

CAT PROBLEMS

If a cat always lands on its feet, and bread always lands jelly side down, what happens to a cat with jelly on its back? Why do cats flick their tails when you talk to them? Why is it easier to lift a cat when it's awake than when it's asleep? Let's tackle some misconceptions and problems *re* our furry feline so-called friends.

CAT FLICK

When cats flick their tails, it is a gesture of contempt. Their low regard for others is matched only by their incredible self-loathing. In an attempt to help cats become less disdainful of themselves and others, they have organized feline self-esteem clinics. Often, early kittenhood traumas emerge as the true source of conflict with dogs, humans, and other cats.

The point to all this? Next time you talk to a cat, if it wags its tail, stop talking. Being codependent to a sick cat is no way for either of you to live.

FELONIUM

Cats weigh more in the dark. This is why it's more difficult to move a cat at night than during the day. A cat's blood, you see, contains felonium. Felonium is photopudorphic; that is, its specific gravity is inversely proportional to ambient light intensity. So during the day your cat's blood is a light, airy froth, and your cat is correspondingly less massive. At night cats are sluggish because lead is flowing through their veins. Also cats are the spawn of Satan, which can't help.

CAT LICKS

Cats are among the most fashion-conscious creatures in the animal kingdom. When a cat licks itself after you pet it, chances are your insensitive petting has ruined your cat's "fur do." This is merely a theory. The other possibility is that your cat is licking itself to show you how you should have petted it, or that it would simply rather do the job itself.

BLACK CATS

You should never attempt to brush a black cat. You are toying with forces beyond mortal comprehension. Black cats are actually a feline version of a black hole, sucking matter and energy into its vortex at nearly the speed of light. If you ever get close enough to brush a black cat and still survive, consider yourself lucky.

DOWNSIDES TO DOGS

DOG HOWLS

A dog howls when it hears a siren because it wishes to share the pain. He knows all too well that the siren means that someone, somewhere is in big trouble. Dogs are living examples of the compassionate spirit Eugene Debs had in mind when he said, "As long as anyone is in prison, I am in prison." Like Debs, the dog is probably a socialist, but unlike Debs, the dog is unlikely to spend time in prison because of it. With the collapse of the Soviet Union the Red scare is finally over. We can all relax, knowing that dogs are simply howling like the hound of heaven, crying out for social justice. A dog's howls are merely ineffectual and cute, so plug your ears and go back to sleep.

DOGS AND MIRRORS

Speaking of superstitions, if a dog breaks a mirror, it is doomed to forty-nine years of bad luck. This is a hard fact. Since this curse exceeds the lifetime of a dog, it necessarily must pass into its next incarnation: the doggy equivalent of eternal damnation. That's why a dog won't get within a mile of a mirror if it can help it.

Have you ever seen a dog looking at itself in a mirror? Cats do it all the time, but dogs? No sir. A dog would rather gnaw a cyanide bone than get near an infernal looking glass. Since canine consciousness lies within the bounds of spirituality rather than Science, I won't attempt to divine the whys and wherefores of this.

DOGS AND CARS

Dogs chase cars because they are trying to tell the drivers of those cars something very important. What that is is something the driver, and Science, will probably never know, because no dog has ever successfully caught a car.

OTHER PETS

Cats and dogs are probably the best of a bad lot. Rabbits, rats, mice, and guinea pigs are best used as meals for large snakes. No family with a plump toddler, however, should tolerate the presence of a boa constrictor in the home. There are smaller reptiles available, like chameleons, tiny alligators, and turtles, but somehow they always escape, to be found next summer as dried-up husks in the lilac bushes.

Tropical fish are an option, but their entertainment value is nil. Some movie stars are adopting small Belgian pigs as pets, but I doubt if this fad will spread into the heartland. If you offer your child a choice of barnyard animals as pets, I have a hunch that the pony will always top the list. Birds are extremely annoying. Anteaters are useful, but uncuddly.

There is, however, one interesting possibility.

Gumby is one of the rare intelligent members of the vegetable family, whose other species include the human-eating triffid, the singing plant from *The Little Shop of Horrors*, the Thing, and Dan

Quayle. Gumby differs from his cousins in being able to move from place to place in a rapid sliding motion. He is the envy of other plants for this, and because he has a pony. Not many plants own ponies. There are those plants who despise Gumby, but most have nothing but respect for him. After all, he is the product of evolution. Any mutation that gets you a TV contract is, in my professional opinion, evolution that works.

TO DO AND SEE

1. Let's take a typical situation involving a typical family. Joe and Jane Avogadro (not their real names), and their two children, Mole and Molecular Weight, rent a house in suburban Bethesda, Indiana. Joe is a foreman at the local Honda warehouse, and Jane is a receptionist just down the street at Mitsubishi. Despite thirteen years of marriage, the Avogadros try to have sex at least once a month, provided they can both stay awake long enough after dinner to do so.

   Because they only rent their home, the Avogadros have never developed the instinctual master/slave relationship that goes with owning property. They've never felt that homeowner's rush. Both Joe and Jane complain of feeling apathetic when it comes to minor home repairs. Neither shows the slightest interest in remodeling a home that they do not own. Are the Avogadros "renting" their way through life, rather than "mortgaging" their children's future in order to claim an itemized rather than standard income tax deduction?
2. Even a psychologist would freely admit that if the Avogadros were to approach their banker with even a modest down payment, the financial wheels could be set into motion to change all this. Should they be worrying about the roof leaking, lying awake at night imagining that the asbestos-covered furnace needs immediate replacement?
3. What about the kids? Condoms are theirs, free for the asking in our public schools, but just let them try to get a Sears credit card without a steady job. We discourage promiscuity among teens while handing

out credit cards to even the most insolvent college student. What lessons do we teach our children by this behavior? Are we cutting off our noses to spite our faces? Are we a nation of lemmings being led off a cliff by craggy-faced Republicans with prostate problems?

4. If you answered yes to any of these questions, have you entered a crisis of faith that will make it hard for you to maintain a property, much less marriage?

5. Mandatory financial and marriage counseling may only postpone the inevitable. Tax incentives and religion can only do so much. It may happen next year, or tomorrow. The whole social fabric of our nation may be ripped like the crotch in a pair of cheap jeans. Will we lose our houses to bankers who don't want them, and our marriages to a lonely and desperate promiscuity?

5

INTIMATE DETAILS

WHAT WE'VE SEEN SO FAR

Far be it from me to come on to you like an Old Testament doomsayer or worse, a modern-day liberal, but I think I've made it quite clear that life as you're living it is a living hell. And you didn't even know it until I pointed it out to you.

There you are, either unemployed or stuck in a job you hate, and trapped in a home with potentially psychotic plumbing fixtures, a home overrun by elves, anteaters, and vicious subterranean humanoids. Not to mention cats.

And children. At least once a week, I'd wager (if I were a wagering man), as you sit at your enormous, battered dining room table, a stack of bills on one side, a meager paycheck on the other, a calculator and you stuck in the middle, your offspring will sneak up behind you to throw Factor X into an already baffling equation: ''Daddy, can I get a tattoo?'' they will ask, or ''Mom, can I go to the heavy-metal-bunjee-jump-body-piercing-rap contest?''

What can you say? After all, you've demanded honesty from your young since the time they were old enough to lie. They feel open enough with you to discuss their hopes and desires. Will you shut them down?

Of course you will. Why? Because you're angry, resentful. You don't know what you want and they do. Do you want to pay those bills? No. Do you want to keep working at your job? Don't be silly. And yet there you sit, reconciling yourself to deeds not worthy of you.

Your children know what they want. They want to have logos etched into their flesh as they listen to white noise, then leap from a great height with a giant rubber band tied around their waist.

Your children know who they are. You don't.

TO CARPET OR NOT TO CARPET

If you have a rug, you may be revealing more about yourself than you'd care to have revealed.

Wall-to-wall carpeting in your home may indicate that you are easily embarrassed by displays of emotion in others.

If you are a throw-rug type of guy or gal, you probably have problems with promiscuity. A spotty, insubstantial commitment to covering the floorboards indicates a deep-seated desire to be all things to all people.

Of course there are those who simply opt for bare floors, which are harder to keep clean because every bit of dirt and dust shows. These people have completely uncluttered subconscious minds—usually found only in newborn babies and TV weathermen.

One thing is sure, if you are dissatisfied with your present floor covering, you will not be happy living in your own skin. How often our home furnishings betray the state of our souls!

VACUUM CLEANER

Nature abhors a vacuum, and many of us have found ourselves at wit's end when a dust-choked Hoover or Kenmore fails to suck carpet lint.

Anger will not unclog an appliance, but a skilled serviceman might. Unfortunately, anyone the least bit talented with his hands took a desk job long ago, and now merely shuffles paper from In box to Out, slowly and steadily forgetting any practical knowledge he acquired over the years.

With the vacuum cleaner we have created a scapegoat for the failings of our homes. Where the carpet sweeper of yesterday was expected only to take the crudest grit from the top of the rug, the modern-day electric vacuum cleaner is supposed to dust the entire house, including venetian blinds and stairs.

Is this what NASA had in mind in early 1965 when they brought the original vacuum canisters back from space? One would have to be foolish, deranged, or both not to notice the sudden and dramatic increase in suction power after that fateful year.

Even the most cursory examination of vacuum cleaner advertising shows the influence of imported extraterrestrial vacuum on home machines. As is so often the case in the sweetheart deals between government and industry, it was the taxpayer who financed ever-increasing profits for vacuum cleaner manufacturers. Free from the regulations imposed by the laws of thermodynamics, they operate under heavy subsidies.

It is this filthy scenario that spurs this Scientist to avoid all dealings with vacuum cleaners. I sold my last machine at a garage sale in 1970. If my floor is dirty, I sweep or mop. If a carpet needs cleaning, I hang it on the line and beat it, just as my father beat the multiplication tables into my head so many years ago.

DUST BUNNIES

The web of the arachnid is low-income housing for a cob or spider, very much like the human's hogan or geodesic dome. The dust bunny, however, is a living creature, its offspring produced when stray socks and lint-trap lemurs mate. Often called nature's fuzzball by good-natured biologists, the dust bunny is a lovable little mammal against whom zealous housecleaners have an unreasonable prejudice. For all our much-vaunted concern over spotted owls and gnatcatchers, here's one endangered species right under our feet, and all we can think to do is sweep it under the rug.

Like our kids.

VARITHANE OR WAX?

Time was, elbow grease and soapy water was all it took to make a floor shine. But then the chemical companies found that people were lazy and insecure enough to want chemistry to do the job for them.

Think of all the layers we impose on the ground beneath our feet. There is a concrete foundation, a subfloor, a finished floor of hard or soft wood, which has been stained and varnished. This is then covered with a layer of wax or plastic, which is in turn covered with a foam pad, and finally a carpet, which is then often treated with chemical shampoos, deodorizers, stain guards, etc.

No wonder we feel out of touch with the real world!

This Scientist prefers to sleep under the open stars, often wrapped in a simple cocoon of newspaper and garbage bags. But even if you have the yearning to escape, the dull Bob inside you won't let you. Instead, you try to placate your playboy Bob with the ludicrous travesty we call home entertainment.

A FEW WORDS ABOUT AUDIO

Radio. Doesn't the word have a certain magic to it? What can I say about radio that hasn't been common knowledge for half a century? And who cares about radio now that we have television? You should, for one.

Long before computer programs there were radio programs. Decades before anyone imagined computers designing other computers, there were regenerative radio receivers. *Radio* is a magic word that describes a magical phenomenon.

Did you know that the personal computer is merely a type of radio? It is when we define our terms. For our purposes, anything that sits on a desk, uses electricity, and has knobs on the front of it is a radio.

Remember a few years back, when we heard the computer industry sing the praises of the personal computer? How it was going to change family life overnight? Soon, Dad would figure the family finances, balance the checkbook, and file the income tax all within a few minutes. Mom would plan the family's menus by calling up an astonishing variety of recipes, with only the leftovers in the fridge as a database. Not only would the computer tell her what to cook and how to cook it, it would tell her how to shop. If the neighborhood supermarket were properly equipped, the computer would actually do the shopping for her.

None of this happened. Today your average family despises the computer. Those old PETs sit in the closet, having failed to sell at the last few garage sales.

No, the advances we've seen in computers have to do with hard disks and laser printers. Some advances. Hard disks are nothing more than floppy disks made in Eastern bloc countries. Laser printers are merely broken antimissile launchers.

So why haven't you been using your home computer as a radio? Because you didn't even notice that it was a radio until I told you. And why haven't you noticed? Simple. Your home computer lacks an antenna. If you were only to jab a wire into the RS-232 port and then toss the wire out the window, you'd find a broad range of AM and FM stations eager to leap from your computer's tiny speaker.

Sure, you'd have to adjust your way of thinking about your computer. Instead of a station-tuning knob, you'll have to use your mouse. And the old band-selection knob, which allowed you to choose from long, medium, and short waves, would be replaced by the computer's function keys.

Listening to Rush Limbaugh berate Democrats from your PC might take some getting used to. Hearing Michael Bolton's whiny upgrades of soul classics erupt from deep inside the disk drive might frighten you with images of lost files and damaged data. But if you dare use your home computer for more than just arcade games, as more than just a fancy typewriter, you'll show others you know the real dope about this computer/radio scam. And, of course, you'll prove that you've read this book.

FADS IN POPULAR MUSIC AND PREVALENT THEORIES IN SCIENCE

At the Sun Studios in Memphis, Sam Phillips knew that something magical was happening that July afternoon in 1955. A nineteen-year-old boy with a greasy ducktail was wailing ''That's All Right Mama'' into Sam's primitive recording equipment. Both the equipment and the singing were simple, crude, and honest.

Within weeks that anonymous teenager would be the hottest singing sensation on the country charts. Who was he? We'll find out, right after this.

A balmy summer evening in the coal country of the Caucasus. The Russian economy might be bankrupt, but there's a wealth of Scientific discovery going on deep under the ground, as millions of gallons of liquid gallium detect the flash of a neutrino exploding as it slams into another subatomic particle at a speed approaching light.

Is there a connection? Ponder this: Is it mere coincidence that modern theories of the so-called new physics fail to account for most of the matter in the universe, while the young Elvis Presley managed to revolutionize music, even though he had no musical training?

Sure, Pat Boone could sterilize a soul number better than anyone since Dick Haymes, but how does that account for the fact that forty years later, no one is quite sure what happened to the music industry when the Hit Parade abandoned the doggy in the window and focused instead on a hound dog? And why do all the bands on MTV simply seem to be pale imitations of Led Zeppelin, a band who did most of their work twenty years ago?

Was Don McLean right? Has the music died? Are neutrinos truly lacking in mass as well as electric charge?

Fortunately, both music and subatomic physics achieve progress through massive infusions of money. Painful as it may be in these times of economic uncertainty, there is a simple solution to most of life's perplexities.

Throw money at the problem.

What if we were to open the Superconducting Supercollider to Texas teenagers and their garage bands? Think of the echo the giant subterranean donut could add to their anemic vocals! It could rival Sam Phillips's famous tape delay, the sound so often associated with all those Hillbilly Cats.

THE STEREO SYSTEM

The word *stereo* comes to us from the ancient Greek. A *steria* was a pair of wooden boxes each containing a *woofa* and a *tweeta*, two porcelain bowls containing raw sound. *Steria* were often stolen and pawned at the Forum, which later became Crazy Eddie's.

Today's modern stereo system is a far cry from the old hi-fi. For one thing, the turntable has largely been replaced by the compact disc player. Vinyl "licorice pizzas" have given way to shimmering holograms, storehouses for massive amounts of digital data.

A word here on the difference between digital and analog. Digital is better. No doubt about it. Digital information is made up of bits or bytes, whereas analog information is just letters and words. There is no comparing the two. Digital is like going to a Sensurround movie, and analog is like reading a cheap paperback.

The heart of your stereo system always was and always will be the amplifier. Let's take a few moments to get to know this most important piece of equipment.

THE AMPLIFIER

There are two types of amplifiers, regenerative and degenerative. A regenerative amplifier feeds some of its output signal back into its own mouth. This is poor hygiene and even poorer Science. Never buy a regenerative amplifier. They're only made in Red China and sold in America under the Sunflower or Happy Boy brand names.

A degenerative amplifier uses the law of entropy to ensure loud and abusive sound reproduction. This is especially suited for most New Wave music. New Age music, on the other hand, will not play at all on a degenerative amplifier. The sounds produced are too wimpy to make it through the amplifier's circuits.

THE CASSETTE RECORDER

Younger brother of the reel-to-reel tape recorder, the cassette recorder began its life as a dictation device. The folks at Norelco, the Norwegian electric shaver company, reasoned that a skinny little tape moving at a snail's pace could do little more than capture the most meager low-fi warblings.

Norelco engineers couldn't have guessed their dictation device would bring audio recording into every home. But then, they hadn't counted on the ferocious determination of Ray Dolby.

A BRIEF HISTORY OF THE TAPE RECORDER

Tape recording began just south of San Francisco, right after World War II. When Bing Crosby and Ted Ampex invented the first reel-to-reel tape recorder, they were really only improving on a system Hitler had devised to help decipher Satanic messages from beyond the veil.

(Today detection of these messages survives only as a hobby for Senate wives and investigative journalists for supermarket tabloids.)

Crosby's interest was to make it possible for him to perform his popular weekly radio show only once, instead of twice for both Eastern and Pacific time zones. Ampex simply wanted to get rich. And Ray Dolby? He only wanted to make an obscure Norwegian dictation device better. He had no selfish motive, no vested interest. "If it works, name it after me," said the shy, self-effacing former house painter from Escondido.

Today the Dolby system is employed in virtually every cassette recorder sold. It also makes movies louder. In layman's terms, Dolby noise reduction uses small pieces of tape to create the illusion of a larger piece of tape, using miniature lasers to create a virtual image of the tape in question. Recording is then done on this hologram. Playback is achieved by projecting this image through a magnifying lens onto the virtual counterpart of the eardrum, the device we call the speaker. Since this ear, or speaker, is hard of hearing, hiss and other defects of the original recording are rendered inaudible.

Ingenious? Yes. Complicated? Somewhat.

And what of the other options on your typical tape deck? Bias. The counter and counter-reset button. Some high-end decks even have a toggle switch marked Source on one end and Tape on the other. What do these switches do?

You don't want to know.

Bias

The high-bias switch does pretty much what its name implies: It increases prejudice to a point where reason breaks down completely. Mob rule. Block busting. Low bias is merely the flip side of the same coin. Affirmative action. Reverse discrimination.

This switch was added as part of a compromise in the Freedom in Piracy Act, passed by Congress in 1965. Certain senators from the South wanted to make sure that tape decks couldn't record soul music. To this day, any attempt to record Marvin Gaye with the high bias switch on results in a warbly rendition of Pat Boone singing underwater.

The high-bias switch will *not* make unsoulful recordings soulful. Simply flipping a switch will not turn Wilson Phillips into Aretha Franklin.

Counter-Reset Button

One should *never* press the counter-reset button. Those numbers are part of the sophisticated accounting system that monitors the many bytes of digital information upon which the entire music industry depends. Musical preference, listening frequency, belief in a Higher Power—all this is encoded and retained so long as you keep your curious fingers *off* the reset button.

Source/Tape Toggle Switch

Fooling around with this switch is potentially even more dangerous. This switch only appears on decks with three heads. If you make a recording without cleaning the heads and the switch is in tape mode, then the second head eats the first head. The third head becomes enraged and bites the ears off the second head. By this point the capstan has gotten involved, and you're lucky if the RIAA roll-off hasn't sounded a silent alarm.

Plan to spend several thousand dollars on legal fees, defending yourself from lawsuits involving copyright infringement. Also kiss your tape deck and the cassette itself good-bye.

THE COMPACT DISC

By now the foregoing is already moot. A large portion of the populace owns at least one compact disc player. Those who don't and never will fall into two groups: folks with hearing damage, and the sturdy iconoclasts who hang onto their gummy eight-track tape players or Montgomery Ward hi-fi's they've had since they went to college in the sixties.

One attribute of our new technology these people are missing out on is the piercing highs and destructive lows a compact disc can put out. Music that can hurt. Yes, the CD player is a weapon, and like most weapons, it should never be pointed at anyone in jest.

In fact, in some states, all compact disc players are sold with a warning sticker that reads "Danger! The heart of this instrument is a laser, just like the ones used in the Former Star Wars defense system, only smaller." This wordy message seemed to have no effect on CD player sales. Most state-of-the-art audio equipment is sleek, miniaturized, and bought by young men. The warning could have read "Watch Out! There's a laser inside just like the ones used in supermarket bar code readers," but that wouldn't have appealed to the average hormone-hopped male.

Of course, you can't just buy the player. You need the discs as well. And they're expensive. This Scientist recommends joining more than one compact disc club. You get up to ten discs for a dollar, with the usual promise to buy more at regular club prices. Of course, you do no such thing. The downside to this behavior is that it can affect your credit rating and the discs they offer are mostly Vivaldi's *Four Seasons* and *Perry Como's Greatest Hits*, with *Jan and Dean, Volume Five* thrown in for the young-at-heart.

But imagine the joy of hearing Perry at full volume, breaking windows with his soporific croon!

TELEVISION

What modern home doesn't have a color TV? Only the poorest of the poor, people who will never read this book. So for statistical purposes we can assume, as the government does, these people don't exist.

Nowadays it's popular to lament the enormous influence television has on the average family by citing how many hours per day the set is on. It may surprise you to learn that Science has a formula that can provide a concrete number for the negative effects television has on your life.

To get that number, simply multiply the number of hours the TV is on per week by the average number of people watching it. Then divide this figure by the number of hours you spend in church multiplied by the number of hours you spend in therapy.

If your family is typical, the number you wind up with should lie somewhere between 20 and 30. This Scientist is aware of one family who had a reading of 450. This was, of course, the famous Nielsen family. Today, unfortunately, this family has been institutionalized.

But don't let fear stop you. If you apply yourself, you can get right in tune with the people who make television. You'll find yourself thinking like they do. Or don't. You'll murmur, "Yes, yes, of course!" as you watch reruns of *Hunter*.

From there, getting along in popular culture will be like swimming downstream. Sure, there will be eddies and whirlpools along the way, but a gentle jog to one side will send you flying right by them. Look, there goes *Mr. Ed*! Watch out for *Rhoda*! No problem. Like the bumper sticker says, "Shit happens." And no matter what comes down, it's over in twenty-two and a half minutes!

SIMPLE DYSFUNCTION

You may have noticed that every time you move to adjust the picture on your television, it adjusts itself. There's a simple explanation for this.

Television is a visual medium. It can only communicate with

you through the picture tube. Experience has shown the television that no matter how outrageous the image it shows you, you'll just assume you're watching a show made in Hollywood. So the television gets your attention by becoming dysfunctional. Like many of us, your television is crying out for attention, for some connection with the rest of society. If you spent a few minutes a day gently stroking your television, it wouldn't need to fail in order to get your attention.

Gently twiddle the knobs while humming the theme from your favorite show. If that doesn't work, threaten to buy another model. Use your imagination! Chances are your TV will reward you with many years of trouble-free service.

ANOTHER DYSFUNCTION

Research has shown that the clothing of television weathermen flickers, while the clothing of anchor people doesn't. I don't wish to alarm you, but Science thinks that Willard Scott may actually exist in more than one dimension at the same time. The fact that weatherpeople speak more inanely and foolishly than other members of television news staffs, sportscasters included, does not indicate that they are playing with less than a full deck but that they're playing more than one game.

It appears to be a fact, proven by weather reports, that other decks and other players exist in other dimensions. Whether this has any practical value for the rest of us remains to be seen. I advise each and every one of you to videotape the next weathercast you see and examine that tape carefully. Does the weatherman appear to be emotionally present? Is he wearing clothing that clashes—say, a plaid jacket with a striped shirt? Do his sentences really make sense, or are they just crude approximations of human communication? This flickering may be just the tip of a virtual reality iceberg.

MR. ED

Mr. Ed was not a horse, but the unfortunate victim of early steroid experiments. A former talk show host, muscle builder Ed M______ found himself unemployable until he turned his horselike appearance and passable Johnny Cash impression into a meal ticket. When the TV show was finally canceled, Ed M______ took a series of odd jobs, including working as a travel agent and managing a hotel. Talking still comes naturally to the garrulous mutant. He has retired in Arizona, and can still be heard muttering, "Oh, Wilbur!" to this day.

THE VCR

Remember the Cargo Cults? Those wacky Pacific Islanders who revered cast-off army items? They built landing strips and wooden replicas of the airplanes they saw in World War II, hoping these totems would bring back all those interesting folks who visited for a while.

Today there's probably some guy in a grass skirt, still sitting in a homemade control tower waiting to guide the gods and their B-52s to a safe landing. We can make fun of him, but we know that these Pacific Island types were onto something.

Take the VCR. Like the dead Elvis or a B-52, it seems to have power over our lives above and beyond what you'd have imagined. It keeps whole families at home, passive, unable to communicate with one another. People who once used the commercial break as an opportunity to come up for air, to sneak in a comment, an opinion, a cry for help, now sit helpless, paralyzed, like a termite hypnotized by the seductive gaze of an anteater.

Believe me, now is the time to get on your VCR's good side. Build a shrine: a few candles, a satin banner, maybe a picture of Dave Garroway or Philo Farnsworth (the real inventor of television, not that sneaky David Sarnoff, who tried to steal the credit for it). Perhaps a slogan on the banner would be nice. How about "All Honor to the Minds Who Created the Medium." That's what they have on the ugliest statue in the world, at Fox Television (formerly Metromedia), in Los Angeles.

THE EXOSKELETON THAT AIMS TO PLEASE

It might surprise you to learn that the VCR is a mutated arthropod. Early prototypes had long spindly legs; they tended to scuttle under the bed and form colonies there, like ungainly spiders, using dust bunnies for nesting material. These colonies, while nonvenomous, gave American consumers the creeping willies.

User-friendly computer technology first allowed bioengineers to eliminate troublesome cistrons in VCR genes, giving us what is today a mere exoskeleton with a mouth.

Its highly specialized diet of low-protein videocassettes is shared with us in what is essentially a "lookie." When ten-year-old boys show each other their mouths full of hot lunch in the school cafeteria, grownups are disgusted. Yet when a legless lobster shows us what it is devouring, we call it home entertainment!

As you can see, audiovisual technology has its repulsive side, which is why this Scientist purchases only laser discs for home viewing purposes. Laser discs are both inorganic and shiny, two definite pluses for any Science-minded couch potato.

SOME FINAL THOUGHTS ON THE VCR

We're all familiar with the Serbian adage "If a man's mind is a mess, then his house is a malodorous pit," but how many of us let such familiarity lead us to contempt? Do we really want a plumber or an architect to fix our home? Or do we want somebody's friend, or in-law, or even a nice guy whose car we waved down as he was driving by to come inside and do the job for free?

We get only what we pay for, my friends, unless it's a free sample in the mail. And when our expectations are unfulfilled, we understandably blame the Realtor. Or the bank. Or our nation's democratically elected government. What do you do if your new siding is warped? Call your congressman. Roof leaks two years after you've had new shingles put on? Get the president on the phone.

In a country where lawyers grow on trees, this mode of thinking can be dangerous. We could end up with a government that works as smoothly as Egypt's. You know how long it takes to get anything done in Italy?

No, we must count our blessings and get on with the business of life. As many a T-shirt, feed cap, and bumper sticker proclaim, "Life's a bitch and then you die"; "When the going gets tough, the tough get going"; "I don't have a drinking problem. I drink. I get drunk. I fall down. No problem." The VCR must be seen in this context. It's just another gregarious stranger we invited into our homes to help fine-tune our life-styles, and now we can't get rid of it. The VCR is a blessing. It's a curse. Like life itself.

Now this.

FAMILY DYSFUNCTION BAROMETER

1. Your teenage daughter comes home four hours late, smelling like a brewery. When you confront her on her tardiness and condition, she laughs in your face and calls you pathetic. At this point you should: (a) Call the police. (b) Slap her in the face and call her a tramp and a hussy. (c) Make an appointment for her to see a psychiatrist. (d) All of the above.
2. You come home from work to find your wife with her head in the oven. You assume that she's merely cleaning, but when she's in the same position an hour later you begin to worry. At this point you

should: (a) Call an ambulance. (b) Recognizing that self-expression is one of the fundamental needs of all persons, wisely leave her alone. (c) Make an appointment for her to see a psychiatrist. (d) Send out for pizza.

3. It's Sunday afternoon and you're watching your favorite sporting event on television. Suddenly your son enters the room and switches the channel to a religious program. You notice that he is wrapped in a bedsheet and there is a glazed look in his eyes. He is wearing eye makeup. At this point you should: (a) Compliment him on his appearance. (b) Hit him as hard as you can. (c) Go buy another television so he can watch his religious programs in private. (d) All of the above.

4. You come home from work and find a note saying that your family has left you. Your husband has run off with a woman half his age and your children have run off to become street people. At this point you should: (a) Turn on the television and watch every public television cooking show you can find. (b) Drink chicken soup from the can as you watch Bradshaw on the family. (c) Begin to read back issues of that magazine you never got around to reading. (d) All of the above, and then some.

THE FAMILY IN CRISIS

So far, I have avoided this subject like the plague, but it can be put off no longer. No denial, here's the cruel truth: If you have a family, make no mistake, it's dysfunctional. Nowadays we're finding out that all of us are Adult Children of Something. It's our job to find out just what that Something is.

As usual, Science comes to the rescue. Just as a master mechanic can diagnose what's wrong with your car just by listening to it, so can a trained Scientist give you an exact and brutally honest analysis of what's wrong with your family. The reason? Science is part of the solution and part of the problem. Not only is Science able to describe the exact nature of familial dysfunction, but Science is actually *a cause* of such dysfunction! Science has provided the technology for everything from digital audio to reproduction of television programs, all of which are specifically designed to keep family members from communicating with one another.

Let's get specific.

Say your teenager is into promiscuity and drugs. Your husband has let his obsession with male pattern baldness interfere with his sleep. Your wife goes from one doctor to another, in search of the attention and compassion you cannot or will not give her. Your youngest child wakes up screaming several times every night. What can you do short of running away?

You must first of all surrender to your own powerlessness. Remember, *dysfunctional* is another word for *normal*. All your attempts to fix those around you will be in vain. Stop judging others and instead rely on a power greater than yourself: the power of Science.

If Science can send a man to the moon, can't it solve your family problems? Every time we flip on a light switch we fully expect an uninterrupted flow of electrons. All we have to do is remember to pay the power bill. Science does the rest. The immutable laws of physics will keep us warm, well-lit, and reasonably comfortable, provided we don't try to run the show by ourselves.

Can't Science do the same with your husband's or wife's newfound disinterest in sex? Or more accurately, in having sex with you? Of course it can, and will, if you invite Science into your bedroom, as well as your home.

Let's take a look at your family.

KIDS

Unfortunately, no home would be complete without kids. Unless you've recently emigrated from some Latin country, that probably means 2.3 kids. But still, these kids need to be born, nurtured, and eventually detained during working hours in one of our school systems.

Let's start at the beginning.

GIVING BIRTH

Even though most Scientists are men and have never personally given birth, they seem to have a great many opinions about how it should be done. If you're a Scientist of any sort, or merely a man, it's your cultural right to continue this arrogant heritage.

Your wife may temporarily fail to appreciate your efforts. Don't become discouraged. This is an emotional time for her. It's best for you to continue doing what you do best, giving advice and staying a safe distance from the grisly reality of childbirth.

DAYCARE

Here again, the Scientific perspective is sorely needed. Years ago, B. F. Skinner incarcerated his own children in a box of his devising. This first attempt at rearing children in a controlled laboratory environment resulted in much negative publicity. You can probably do as much as Skinner did and more, without the publicity. Simply turn your entire home into a laboratory. Install one-way mirrors through which you can monitor all activity. Replace anything soft with something hard, anything that could absorb or muffle with polished stainless steel.

The more sterile your home becomes, the more accurately your children will replicate Skinner's data of half a century ago. You see, kids haven't changed. Our ways of rearing them have. What with disposable diapers and Mr. Rogers, Transformers, Barney, and Flintstone vitamins, kids today have a hard time conforming to a norm. And when you're statistically deviant, true deviance cannot be far behind.

EDUCATION

Our children must avoid deviance at all costs. A sterile home environment goes a long way toward preparing our children to fit into the work force as adults, but it still cannot teach them the complete passivity necessary for long-term employment. Someone must teach the art of showing up on time, sitting still, and keeping papers neat.

PUTTING IT TOGETHER

Does a sick society produce a sick family, or does a sick family produce a sick society? Well, which came first, chicken or road? Such speculation leads nowhere. We must look to the future and act, otherwise Science, government, and industry will act for us. They will descend on the American family like a swarm of locusts. They will teach our children to conform to national specifications. Like semiconductors on a circuit board, our children will stand in neat rows, soldered in place by underpaid women overseas. And if a unit fails to perform, we will have Quality Control to ensure that it is tossed out quickly, before its failure can damage units farther down the line.

This scenario should bring a relieved smile to the lips of the Daddy Bob inside you, and a shudder to the spine of the Playboy Bob within. And there's our national consciousness in a nutshell: Hercules holds his nose as he wrestles with the droppings of the Augean stables, and Pandora swats the buzzing evils as they swarm out of the box. When they back into each other inadvertently, they are so conflicted they cannot apologize, but must turn on each other with a snarl, like two vicious kittens trapped in a grocery bag.

And that is where most Americans' ''heads are at'' here at the end of the twentieth century, wincing and grinning like lovestruck teens at a slasher movie.

FYI...

"Wedding at night, lawyer's delight."

So goes the old saw, and it's true. People who get married at night are always divorced by dawn. There is something in darkness that abhors a marriage. Without the sunshine of hope and mutual appreciation, even the most passionate lovers become bitter enemies shortly after exchanging vows. Studies of marriage survival rates and times of ceremony indicate that the hour of 10:00 A.M. produces the most lasting unions. Those who say "I do" between the hours of 2:00 A.M. and sunrise not only greet the dawn single, but often through the bars of a jail cell. Yes, one irrational act begets another. Before you know it, you're calling your lawyer to arrange both bail and the Big D. If anyone ever asks you to marry him or her after the sun goes down, cross yourself and run away as fast as you can.

"The younger the child, the more powerful the scream." Any new parent can nod appreciatively at the truth of this, the so-called Baby Huey Axiom. But take heart. Even though a newborn's cry can cause cerebral hemorrhages, its power fades with time. By age two most children are merely annoying.

Since the American family has 2.3 children, you may wonder what ultimately becomes of the .3 child.

He or she usually becomes a television personality. Sally Jesse, Oprah, even Maury Povich are all examples of the determination and gumption that allows a fraction of a person to rise to the top of the heap! Geraldo outdid them all. Starting with only .000001 of a personality, he achieved near worldwide notoriety in just the last decade. Those of us who were gifted with more at birth need to compare our lot to these and take stock of ourselves while there's still time.

I receive many letters from couples who have been married more than ten years, wondering why their spouses have never risen above the third Chakra in their communication. A wife requests that husband meditate with her, but he just wants to watch television or nap. A husband tries to talk about spending habits with his wife, but she refuses to lift her head from the latest issue of *Vanity Fair.* What can these couples do to maximize their relationships?

My advice? Give up. The chance of anything changing between you and your spouse after ten years of marriage is one in ten billion. You'll have a much better chance of changing your expectations. Ask yourself why you want a maximum relationship instead of, say, a nice car. Let's not forget income property or an extended vacation in an exotic locale. Even better, an extended vacation that doubles as work so it's tax deductible. Take a tip from an indifferent spouse and reevaluate your priorities now, while there's still time.

It's useful to remember that all teenagers naturally produce an EEG pattern Scientists call white noise. We've been able to determine that the average teenager has a complete change of thought every 4.5 nanoseconds. This goes a long way toward explaining why the average high school teacher retires after three years. If you're looking for an occupation that offers early retirement without benefits, you might want to check out secondary education.

THE SCIENTIST WITHIN

An Oprah or a Donahue would be what young people call "in your face" about now, waving a slim microphone like a magic wand and insisting that you share the details of your most intimate life with an audience of millions. That would be fine if you were a Man Who Dresses Like a Woman or The Woman Who Loves Him and I had a microphone, but we're going after something different here.

Mere intimacy means nothing to me. Any of my ex-wives can attest to that. What I am interested in is honesty. Gut-level honesty. I've already shown you the dangers and, yes, wonders both natural and unnatural inside the walls and under the roofs of the homes around us. I've told you how the economy works and what kind of work you ought to be looking for. I've shown you, painstakingly, how Science can improve your life if you are willing to have trained technicians conducting your most personal and private events.

But I don't need a microphone, a television crew, and a studio audience to see the beads of sweat gathering on your forehead. I can sense you balking. "Men and women in lab coats standing in every doorway?" you're thinking. "Dr. Science, I'm sorry, the price of inner peace is too high."

Don't worry. Dr. Science understands. As a matter of fact, to be brutally honest, you *don't* need highly educated observers monitoring your daily lives to achieve *satori*. You have to find those observers within. Forget the inner child! Throw that rug rat out with the bath water!

What we're after here is something larger, and simpler. We're talking about micromanaging your own psyche, about unleashing your Personal Scientist.

But first, some sleeping tips.

HOW TO SLEEP

Even though gravity shortens us when we stand, and we gain our greatest height while lying down, curiously, in most homes, doors tend to be taller than beds.

Why this is, Science does not know.

What we do know is that sleep, like anything that seems effortless, is hard work. It is an art, one in which diligent study will pay, and pay handsomely.

Although the need for sleep varies considerably, all humans need some sleep. (I am that rare exception which proves the rule.)

The exact need for sleep depends largely upon IQ and character. A wholesome and innocent babe, for instance, will sleep most of the day. An erratic genius will only catnap between brilliant yet twisted experiments.

Many drugs either combat or enhance the body's ability to sleep. Caffeine and its antithesis, Sominex, are naturally occurring substances that war for the body's ability to reach a true alpha state. When one has truly risen above the need to reach an alpha, or "near death" state, then one truly begins to live.

Few dare to live life to the max. Few are willing to down pot after pot of thick, black java. Rare is the individual who can stomach the painful stomach, weather the jitters, focus his eyes amidst distracting flashes, and breathe deeply when it feels like his heart is fluttering up around his throat.

To sleep, perchance to dream. Dreaming is, of course, the real payoff in sleeping. But isn't cable television just as soothing? Sure, it's a bit more expensive, but isn't time money? This Scientist would rather work round-the-clock if need be, and pay for the premium movie channels when it's time to cut some slack.

But there are many non-habit-forming ways to induce sleep. You yourself may be one of them. If you've ever noticed that people often seem to nod off while you're talking to them, your body could be emitting what biologists call a narcopheme ombulator. This is an easily synthesized, *marketable* chemical used to help insomniacs. You could make money off this condition, if you don't mind making a living as a sleepless, anxious bore.

Many pheromes are sex-linked, and yours could be as well. Or perhaps you produce the chemical in some odd place, like your hair roots or your ear canals. The only way to find out is to submit yourself to rigorous and thorough testing. It's expensive, painful, and inconvenient (some tests last a month!), but worth it—unless your idea of a good time is watching others sleep.

STORAGE

Now we enter the realm of dreams, the waking dream that we call our private lives: storage and storage-retrieval systems.

No home is complete without room for storage. Whether it's an overstuffed closet, a dusty attic, or a clogged basement, there are the reliquaries of past glory, shrines to objects we dare not part with for fear of losing our very identities. Like a fine wine, the stuff of our lives only mellows with age. And like ectoplasm, it haunts us with bittersweet memories.

Rare indeed is the soul with the courage to clean out that closet, attic, or basement. Who would want to see his or her past stare accusingly from a Dumpster?

It is said that when Gandhi died, his earthly possessions amounted to a pair of sandals, a pair of spectacles, and a single copy of *Jonathan Livingston Seagull*. We modern consumers want to make darn sure this fate doesn't befall us.

Instead, like the ancient Pharaohs, we accumulate huge mounds of goods to sustain us on our voyage to the underworld. So this is the true function of our storage areas, to ensure our rank in the afterlife.

THE WATER HEATER

"You're in hot water now!" scolds an angry mother, teacher, or wife. Just what is it about hot water that makes women use it to threaten their children, students, and spouses?

We know certain facts about hot water. It makes bathing tolerable. It can scald; it can burn. Look at what Gloria Grahame and Lee Marvin did to each other in *The Big Heat*! Hot water can be a friendly helper or a deadly enemy. But where does this schizophrenic substance come from?

The water heater itself is a cylinder tucked away in a musty corner of your basement. One can easily distinguish it from, say, the furnace. The furnace is a box, and is much bigger than the cylinder.

Although their external sizes may vary, both the furnace and the water heater have the same interior. Their external shapes vary only because building codes demand it. Otherwise homeowners would confuse the two objects, since they know intuitively water heaters and furnaces are the same thing.

Your average handyman could easily modify one device to do both jobs, but then where would your Industrial Profit Index go? Straight to hell. Yet, oddly enough, that's what we're dealing with here. Hell. Yes, the water heater and the furnace occupy the third and fourth circles of hell, respectively.

The first circle of hell is going to a social gathering, at which your hosts suggest that you all spend the evening watching the entire series of *thirtysomething*, which they've thoughtfully videotaped. The second level of hell is eating in a Mexican restaurant in Iowa.

We will not be examining these levels of pain at this time (see Levels of Hell in the Appendix). No, we will move on to the third and fourth circles of hell. At last count there are over 6,543 circles in the seemingly endless spiral of hell. We will make no attempt to list them now.

This Scientist rejects the lure of hot water and its many snares. Casual investigation and a gut feeling I just can't dismiss suggest that *agua caliente* is to blame for many modern-day ills, including poor posture, impotence, premature graying and baldness, and a whiny "gimme" attitude, to mention a few.

Who will bring America back to its senses?

Let me use this book as a megaphone to call America back from the third circle of hell. Come back to the invigorating cold shower. Come back to your senses. Through chattering teeth, shout, "Gee, this ain't so bad!" Eschew hot water, grin and bear it. If your lips are blue, then whatever passes them must be the unvarnished truth.

PHOTO ALBUMS

If you're like most of us, then you store your old photo albums within a few feet of the water heater. This is a subliminal attempt to scald family members for whom you feel hidden but very real resentments.

The basement is a dreary place, home of molding dirty laundry, kitty litter pans, lime-encrusted dehumidifiers, and odd pockets of dryer lint. What better sarcophagus for old photographs?

Chances are there's an old slide projector down there as well, and the carousels of slides you haven't seen in fifteen years are packed at the bottom of a soggy cardboard box. Piled on top of that are envelopes full of photos that never quite made it into an album.

To some degree, this explains why amateur photographers are so often sluggish and depressed. Lifetimes of soul-stealing have left them bound with invisible cords to the shallow lives of tens of thousands of family and strangers.

Oddly enough, it is this harboring of frozen images of relatives that binds us to the wreckage of our past. The greater the collection of old photographs, slides, and home movies, the less free we are to move and grow. And once the reality-based craze passes from the television waves, all the unsent tapes to *America's Funniest Home Videos* or *Cops* will also find their way here, to take their rightful place in the glut of reminiscence.

WASHER AND DRYER

Frequently, our clothes are washed and dried in full view of the very mementoes that seemingly give our life meaning. What do we think as we sit through the cycles, thumbing through skimpy magazines, surrounded by our past and confronted by the never-ending damp circle of the present?

As we stand before our dirty laundry, which Bob are we? Is it the playboy or supermodel who cleanses personal items? Is it the family man or supermom who preserves precious memories? Or are both commingled, as we stand there (sitting in my case—my weight does not permit prolonged vertical behavior), watching the underwear spin, watching the relics gather dust?

TO DO AND SEE

THE DR. SCIENCE HOME-DWELLER STRESS CALIBRATOR

Directions: Rate Each Answer on a Scale of 0 ("Not at All") to 4 ("Get Away from Me")

During the past week, how much did you notice:

	Not 0	Sort of 1	More 2	Lots 3	Go Away 4
1. That your head is enclosed in mud or a pillow of some kind.					
2. A cheeselike lump in back of throat.					
3. Palpitations, twitches.					
4. Inappropriate comments at dinner table.					
5. Hot flashes, cold sweats.					
6. A dwarf or monkey watching you just beyond your line of sight.					
7. A sudden compulsion to buy aluminum foil—rolls and rolls of it.					

	Not 0	Sort of 1	More 2	Lots 3	Go Away 4
8. That bones have been replaced by pudding.					
9. People hiding under desks when you come by.					
10. You had difficulty in humming.					
11. A thinly veiled contempt for you among family members.					
12. An urge to dismantle all appliances to "see what makes 'em tick."					
13. Persistent ideas, thoughts, impulses, or images that are intrusive, unwanted, senseless, and/or repugnant.					
14. That you couldn't stop humming.					
15. Feeling that your nose is receding into your face.					
16. An urge to take up a musical instrument of some kind, or write a "bluesy" type of song.					
17. That you no longer recall the name of your best friend from fifth grade.					
18. That your neighbors are all Satanists, or Scientologists, or members of some secret religion you can never hope to understand.					
19. Diarrhea, flatulence, halitosis, postnasal drip.					

	Not 0	Sort of 1	More 2	Lots 3	Go Away 4
20. Rigidity and quivering in lower limbs.					
21. A feeling that something awful is just about to occur.					
22. A feeling that something awful has just occurred.					
23. Bills.					
23. You hate your job.					
24. You hate your family.					
25. Your house is a living entity that wishes to devour you.					
26. Elvis is alive.					
27. Wistful urge to return at once to Indiana.					
28. Jane Pauley doesn't seem as into it as she used to be.					
29. Fingernails are too long.					
30. Water sometimes tastes bad.					
31. Metallic taste when eating certain vegetables.					
32. Robots, everywhere you look, robots.					
33. That Democrats are alarmingly susceptible to bribery.					
34. That the color orange makes you nervous.					
35. You've never read Dickens, Dostoyevski, or *Don Quixote,* and you can't bring yourself to feel bad about it.					

	Not 0	Sort of 1	More 2	Lots 3	Go Away 4
36. You feel bad about not feeling bad.					
37. You don't know what "adult contemporary" means.					
38. You've never been asked to participate in an opinion poll.					
39. Tomatoes don't taste like tomatoes anymore.					
40. You don't understand what George Will is trying to say.					

CHAPTER 6

EDUCATION AND HOME ENTERTAINMENT

THE LINK THAT DEFIES ANALYSIS

For years educators and has-been television producers have been trying to convince themselves and the general public that television possesses educational potential.

There is no such thing as educational television. The two concepts are mutually exclusive. Television does not instruct or educate. It coerces. Like an annoying and dimwitted relative, it sits in the corner telling stories that are sometimes mildly amusing, if you have nothing better to do.

We may also do well to ask ourselves, "Is education really possible?" Does forcing children to sit down facing a wall (or each other if they're at a private school) really introduce new ideas into their brains?

As an attendee at many schools, this Scientist can affirm the veracity of the old hacker's maxim "Garbage In, Garbage Out." Twenty-odd years of enforced matriculation have left me with a strong disgust for other people's educational theories. If you, the

reader, have spent thousands of hours inside the Skinner Box we call the classroom, then you too probably have a portion of resentment against schooling.

Let us combine our disgust and resentment, fusing them into one bitter lump which we can use to bash in the doors of Horace Mann!

THE SO-CALLED FAILURE OF OUR SO-CALLED EDUCATIONAL SYSTEM

We've all heard ceaseless blather about the tragedy of our schools. We've all been wondering why Johnny can't read. Much of our tax money has been spent on useless seminars, workshops, and measurement of this perceived problem. This is truly astounding, in light of the fact that things have never gone more smoothly!

We have to remember the purpose of education: to prepare our future citizens for the opportunities that await them once they are released from mandatory participation in primary education.

And what are those opportunities? Minimum-wage jobs in food service. Insurance or real estate sales. Telemarketing. Is it any wonder that education seems more like incarceration than the intoxication provided by a close encounter of the thinking kind? And teachers are doing nothing to help.

THE LESSON PLAN

If you've ever had the misfortune to teach for a living, you know the necessity of having an approved lesson plan before you enter the classroom. Far from being a burden, however, creating and selling the lesson plan to your superiors is one of the joys of teaching that remains in today's schools. It can make teaching like filing your income taxes and quelling a prison riot, all in one simple step!

Yes, it's easy, and fun to do.

Copy the following, changing the particulars to suit your personality, and you can go on autopilot for the rest of the semester, perhaps even the rest of your career.

8:30 A.M. Enter the classroom, and glance at the students as they noisily socialize at their desks. Braving a momentary wave of nausea, you crack open the textbook. Suddenly it all seems so meaningless, so hopeless. As you stifle the intense desire to bolt for the door—

The bell rings. All eyes turn to you. The ball is in your court.

Fortunately you have a plan. This plan. Tell them to get out a notebook, sharpened pencil, calculator or slide rule, protractor, and compass. Tell them it is their job to create, using only Venn diagrams, a comprehensive analysis of Western Culture from A.D. 1046 to 1946.

All eyes will be on you. In the shocked silence, as they roll their eyes and mumble under their breath, you will hear the whine of your nervous system as it competes with the rapid pumping of your heart.

Bad cop suddenly turns nice. You offer to help. "What about the twelfth-century religious music of Hildegard of Bingen?" you suggest. "How did this music influence, say, the Nazi occupation of the Netherlands?"

A few of the brighter students go right to work. Others engage in furious bouts of nose-picking, while still others closely examine their hair.

Of course, the real trick is to keep them subjugated to your absolute authority. When the initial shock has softened, you need to reenforce your dominance. Experience has shown nothing does this like humming.

As you pace the front of the classroom, begin to hum a simple tune, preferably in a minor key. If you catch someone looking at you, stop humming and stare at that person. Put everything you have into that stare. Hold it for thirty seconds, then abruptly go back to humming.

9:20 A.M. The bell rings. Have the students hand in their papers as they silently file out of the room. When they are gone, throw their papers away.

At the next class session, tell them their work was so poor you decided to give them another chance. Then repeat the above, with as little variance as possible.

No matter what your teaching load, this plan will work six times a day, five days a week, semester after semester.

You'll find what thousands of classroom veterans have known for years: Teaching is the easiest thing in the world! You just have to dodge bullets and have the stomach for it.

The fact is, most educators are already asleep, imagining a retirement far away from waxed linoleum and ink-stained Formica. How often is the classroom a collection of individuals, each mentally projecting in vastly different directions! Physically they are pinned to desks in a line, but Johnny's mind is on a South Sea island, Sharon's at the Winter Prom, and Mr. Johnson's is back at the bordertown night club, the one he visited on spring break back in graduate school.

IS THERE ANY HOPE FOR EDUCATION?

Of course not. But there is hope for society, if we can come up with a more attractive and useful way of incarcerating our young people. After all, economists have long pointed out that our unemployment rates could reach fifty percent if teenagers were out there competing with the rest of us for jobs that require a fifth-grade education.

What about a young people's work project? Send them all to camp in western Nebraska or eastern Montana. There they will forge a new civilization from the ground up. It will give them self-esteem, that precious commodity the lack of which psychologists insist is the root of all our troubles.

Hollywood has also found a use for teenagers: They put them in movies, where their posing and posturing can substitute for acting. In Hollywood they can preen and strut, painfully conscious of their hair, and win the empathy of millions of their fellow nonactors, watching them in theaters or at home.

Unfortunately, there are only so many openings in this field, and there are a lot of teenagers; 99.99 percent of them end up watching .01 percent of their peers earn more money for a few weeks' work than most of us do in a lifetime.

So all right then, it's back to school. What can be done?

A WORD OF WARNING

Before we get to some hard lessons, it is my duty to remind you that it is a felony to induce a minor to become a Scientist. Thirty years ago, of course, it was compulsory to induce the young to embrace our friend the atom, to jump on the post-Sputnik bandwagon and flap their slide rules toward Progress and a better tomorrow.

Well, look at the mess we've made since then. I think you have to agree with those legislators who've called for stiff penalties for minor Scientists—compulsory jail time without possibility of parole. Only a chosen few are capable of handling the responsibilities that come with being a Scientist. The few, the chosen—I'm one of 'em.

STUDY HABITS

If you want information to really stick to your ribs, pay close attention to this section. Remember: *Studying* is a self-directed educational act. It is to learning what masturbation is to sex between consenting adults. Like its glandular counterpart, studying is more enjoyable and effective in uncomplicated solitude. Classroom meetings or private tutorials can leave a student unwanted, a shy wallflower out of place at the orgy.

In order to study effectively, must one be undistracted? Most teachers would say yes. Most teachers would tell you that you can't even *attempt* to conjugate the verbs of a foreign language while watching MTV or engaging in a conjugal act. You can't hope to master the subjunctive tense or find out when that train leaves for Barcelona if you're busy ordering a pizza—that's the assumption of our education cabal. They want you to think that a serious yet relaxed, focused sense of purpose is an absolute necessity. It is this out-of-date pedagogy that's sending us to hell in a handcart.

That's because the powers-that-be don't need teenagers any more. Ever since Science discovered laboratory animals, the teen has become useless. If antivivisectionists are ever successful in stopping animal research, though, Science may call upon the teenager again. In that event, Congress has authorized a new *sub*-sub-minimum wage, which would enable teens to earn pocket change for smokes, gum, and Satanic music for their Japanese-made personal stereo systems. By that time, unfortunately, grownups may no longer have the knowhow needed to lure teens into maturity.

There are few pathways into the mind of the average adolescent, and those are clogged with beer nuts and sunscreen. I'm not talking about the ear canals now—those are usually open, unless the outer ears are covered by headphones. Researchers recently tried gaining access to the average college student's mind by putting subliminal messages on cassette tapes. It was found that no matter the message content, the resulting behavior change always involved either pizza or beer consumption.

That's why, if you wish to promote good study habits, it's an excellent idea to have plenty of coffee, carbonated beverages, chips, and candy on hand. These help the mind call time out, and avoid intimacy with the subject matter. The mind is comfortable in ignorance, and does not want to rush headlong into unfamiliar surroundings. ''Feeding the face'' helps postpone this.

And eventually, almost miraculously, study leads to knowledge. Even the most half-hearted, distracted student must eventually learn something from school.

How? Sociologists and educational psychologists believe it has to do with caffeine and sugar intake, combined with massive amounts of sheer repetition. Plus, the human mind has a tiny yet powerful ally.

The proto-brain is located just behind the right ear, housed in a walnut-sized gland called the Mons Ignoramus. Proto-brain is entirely responsible for marshaling and directing all newfound knowledge. Even when the rest of your brain is asleep, proto-brain prowls the empty hallways of your mind, a restless insomniac, muttering non sequiturs and looking for the bathroom.

While your conscious mind watches *Donahue*, and your autonomic nervous system directs the semiconscious act of snacking, proto-brain scans the myriad facts, opinions, and assorted collected ignorance man has reached by this, the last decade of the century. Proto-brain is searching for a place to roost, and eventually it will find it. There will be a homecoming of sorts, I predict. Once again, new generations will return to that delusional self-satisfaction that allows us to believe we're progressing, despite every evidence to the contrary.

So there is a learning curve as supple and extreme as a fifteen-year-old's posture. But what about those go-getters who not only do their homework, but do it at school? Aren't those polite, well-groomed students who are alert and eager to learn a liability in the subliminal-assimilation educative process I've described above? Sure they are. And they're friendless too. Only a wonk loves a wonk, and wonks are too busy studying to take time out for love.

But more important, what do you call homework if you do it at school? My advice is don't call it anything. You'll only call attention to yourself. You should be pretending to listen to your teacher during the hours you're in school. During my time in the classroom I perfected a glazed stare that I would cast in the teacher's general direction, a kind of Zen meditation that allowed my mind to drift wherever it chose as long as my seat was securely anchored behind my desk. Sometimes, of course, I let my mind wander too far, and my mortal coil would shuffle to the linoleum, not unlike a Slinky, attracting unwanted attention from my so-called instructor. So if you do your homework at home and your meditation at school, you just may amount to something. You might even achieve *satori* by sixth grade. I know I did.

A NOTE FOR PARENTS

As you know, the theory of relativity describes the interchangeability of space and time. If you're a parent and your children are leaving for college soon, you don't need less space but you do need more time—to earn the money to pay for their education. You might want to take a look at Einstein's theory. It could help you out.

If on the other hand you don't want to be burdened by the paradoxes of energy/mass conversion (not to mention the plutonium you'd have to keep in stock), try to get your children into a La Place transformation. This is a completely free program administered through the Federal Department of Higher Mathematics. It will turn all variables into constants, and then through some simple paradigm shifts and a great deal of statistical deviation, either turn your children back into kindergartners, or make them completely self-sufficient. Sure, you have to fill out some forms, but believe me, it beats student loans any day.

OUTMODED LEARNING TOOLS

MULTIPLE-CHOICE TESTS

Much has been written, most of it useless, about how to guess intelligently when faced with a question that goes right past you. Even the sharpest of minds faces such questions, and the challenge of which little dot or candle to fill in with the number-two pencil looms ominously.

Is the best random answer always "E: None of the above"? What about filling in the dots to make a picture?

To answer this question about answering questions, we hired several test-preparation experts to let us in on their trade secrets. Most of them, under the pressure of even the most insubstantial stipend, admitted that they use the faces of cartoon characters to form patterns for their answers. In fact, the SAT has licensed the likenesses of Walt Disney characters for this purpose, and the ACT has a similar deal with Hanna-Barbera.

A tip: Snow White and Yogi Bear are off-limits, but the rest are fair game and often used. Warner Bros. has balked at letting its Looney Tune characters be employed in such a manner, but is rumored to be signing a similar deal with the LSAT.

THE ALPHABET

After more than a million years of lingual evolution, the alphabet gradually emerged from the pecking order we call language. There is no human design behind the arrangement of words in a dictionary. *These words have arranged themselves*. Alphabetization then paved the way for file cabinets, address books, and card catalogues. Many frauds and several cultures have tried to claim credit for inventing the alphabet, but the truth is, it invented itself. And we are still its slaves.

ARITHMETIC

Unless you've had the spiritual training necessary to become a professional mathematician, you should *never* try to distinguish a rational number from an irrational one. The only other thing you need to remember is there can't be a countable subcover of an open cover of a subset of a space whose topology has a countable base. Keep that in mind and you'll do all right.

PHYS. ED.

Those who run for health are only running away from themselves. They are acutely aware of this from a place hidden deep in their brains, probably the Pons Athleticus, an organ that serves as the mind/body interface. The intense realization of this conflicted act causes the grimace they wear as they run. This mask of pain is really a silent cry for help, but its sheer hideousness keeps all but the most compassionate paramedic from tackling the problem.

Speaking of tackling, how can you stop a runner short of tackling him mid-stride? As anyone who's had the misfortune to play football or rugby knows, this is a risky business for both parties. This

Scientist remembers all too well the acute discomfort of a separated shoulder received one crisp autumn afternoon during an informal skirmish at the research park.

Experiences like that finally forced me to make and keep a vow of perpetual indolence. Although my weight has ballooned to gargantuan proportions, I retain a youthful flexibility and vigor, at least cranially.

We only have so much energy and time to expend. How we manage these resources depends on our personalities and unconscious needs. Thanks to countless hours on the analyst's couch, I am fully in touch with my unconscious mind, and can prioritize my life accordingly. In fact, I can go so far as to say that I have finally succeeded in bringing total unconsciousness into all my affairs. I'm not bragging, I'm just saying what's real for me. With any luck, someday you'll be able to do the same.

GEOGRAPHY

Geography is still important, believe it or not. While latitude is ultimately more important than longitude when making a map, attitude is more important than both. How many captains have stood inebriated on the for'ard deck, smarting from some imagined injustice as their tankers ran aground on the shoals? Sure, it helps to know where you are, but the question of where you're coming from sometimes means much, much, much more.

OUTMODED EQUIPMENT

PENS

As the compact disc is to the LP, so is the pen to the pencil. It wasn't long ago that Americans carefully husbanded tiny slivery stubs of wood that encircled number- two graphite. We painstakingly erased errors, blew the eraser shavings into a cupped hand, and carefully placed the leavings on the compost heap.

Today we write any damn thing that pops into our head, scratching phrases out with willy-nilly abandon. If we don't like what we've written, we crumple the page and throw it at the dog with a cry! Fact: If we could take back all the angry letters to the editor that appear in one typical American day, an entire rain forest would reappear.

That's the downside. The upside? Well, there's an upsurge in self-expression. People from all walks of life, of every political stripe, are wrinkling their brows over their thesauri as they cultivate derivative prose styles and nurture their rage over the plight of the homeless and/or welfare frauds. And jobs. Jobs in the lumber industry, jobs creating greeting cards, and most of all, jobs making pens. Let's take a brief overview.

Fountain Pen

The modern fountain pen had its origins in the quill pen, the writing utensil of choice for more than a thousand years. Little more than a modified goose feather, this pen was used by our forebears either to draft important documents or to form the conspicuous signature we call the John Hancock, for reasons which, alas, are lost in the obscurity of history.

In the nineteenth century, the feather nib was replaced by a sturdy steel comb, for reasons which probably had more to do with the shrinking goose population in industrialized areas and the invention of the pocket than with organized pressure brought to bear on scribes by the powerful steel industry. There were some holdouts, like Abe Lincoln, who preferred penning his thoughts in charcoal on the backs of shovels, but this made filing unwieldy (and bookbinding impossible!). This practice was also a contributing factor to both the Great Shovel Shortage of 1858 and the Secretarial Riots of 1859, both directly linked to Abraham Lincoln's bouts of depression.

But I digress. As with all pens (until 1956), the fountain pen took advantage of the interface between *surface tension* and *capillary action*, allowing a writer to form tiny black or blue puddles on an otherwise blank piece of paper. When dry, these little puddles formed hieroglyphs which could often be interpreted by others.

Today, government permits are needed to own fountain pens, which are only used to sign official state documents. After a typical signing, the fountain pen is taken to a special room, where it will later be placed under glass and shipped to a presidential library. True, some feminists and other sensitive types use fountain pens for *calligraphy* (flowery writing) or to jot down their deepest thoughts in aromatic journals. But these people are taking the law into their own hands, and if there's any justice in the world, they will someday be brought before the bar to answer for their actions.

Ballpoint

A tiny little steel ball bearing is crammed into the hollow end of a tube, where it attracts ink, in order to smear it all over a blank surface, such as a piece of paper or a white shirt pocket.

Roller Ball

The roller ball pen operates under the same principles as the ballpoint pen, except the tiny ball is made of disposable plastic rather than steel. It tends to skip, rather than smear. Like the ballpoint pen, the roller ball pen is easily disposed of. A quick flick of the wrist and it's gone.

Felt Tip

The felt tip pen inverts the process of the old-fashioned quill pen. Where the quill pen waved its feather proudly in the air, as ink flowed down to the writing surface, the felt tip places the *feather itself* on the writing surface, to make it write through sheer brute force.

The plastic housing of the felt tip conceals several yards of once gay plumage, now clogged and clotted with ink. Thus, the felt tip is the cruelest of pens. Still, it isn't as leaky as the others mentioned, and again, is highly disposable.

ELECTRIC TYPEWRITER

Inside every electric typewriter there are sixty-three miniature robots, fueled by pure electricity. They are concealed deep inside the typewriter so you can't see them, even if you look for them in the gaps between the keys. When your electric typewriter breaks down, that means the little robots are sick. When you call the typewriter repairman, you're really calling a robot doctor. If he tells you he has to take the typewriter into the shop, that means he can't do anything to help you because all the little robots are dead.

Of course, I'm exaggerating, but you can see why most people have switched to digital.

LIQUID PAPER

Ever wonder what Liquid Paper's made of? Well, have you ever stepped on a snail and seen that white goo come out? That has nothing to do with what Liquid Paper's made of. I was just making sure you were paying attention.

The fact is, Liquid Paper is a fungus, a relative of slime mold, manufactured in library basements. Book rot is collected as it drips from the moldy stacks upstairs, then shipped to Hong Kong, where it is mixed with various herbs (florabunda, nightbane), and Elmer's. It is then shipped by junk to Minnesota, where it is bottled by bored college students with attitudes bigger than their earning potential. So the next time you buy a bottle, marvel at all that goes into it! Then throw it away. Its time has come and gone.

LANGUAGE

When they die, languages disintegrate into syllables, phonemes, and guttural stops. It's possible to wipe out an entire language in less than a century. The English did it with Cornish back in the nineteenth century. Right now many television shows are attempting to destroy the English language. Soap operas employ a vocabulary of only a few hundred words, and the actors spend at least a third of the time repeating each other's names.

USA Today is coming out with a special daily that is all pictures and graphs, augmented only by a few words such as *Wow, Yep*, and *Huh*. From a Scientific perspective it's just another example of entropy in action. Join it.

COMPUTERS

The reason computers count in the binary system is because they only have two fingers. We, born with ten, would be better off with computers that use a decimal counting system. The first computer, incidentally, was invented in 1664 by thc Sri Rav Gopal, a mathematician in Calcutta, who devised a wood and India-rubber computer based on the number of fingers on the many hands of Quishnu, the Hindu god of irrefutable logic. I believe the number was 64,280. Not much work got done with that computer, though it was beautiful to look at. The English confiscated it sometime in the nineteenth century and turned it into a loom, which they exported to Northern Ireland, where it was used to make shirts and enslave the local populace.

ONE SCIENTIST'S FINAL WORD

After years of study, another Scientist steps from the forge; his or her every subsequent result will be gained through grit, gumption, determination, and lavish expenditure of your tax dollars. In return for trustworthiness, the true Scientist is given gifts, such as the ability to synthesize intelligence in a handy credit card–sized container. I myself have not received my gift, but when I do, I'll donate all royalties to my favorite charity, the Old Scientist's Home in Rocheport, Missouri. This is my pledge to you.

TO DO AND SEE

Are you a Scientist? You may be one already, you know. If you are, your problems may be over. Check it out.

1. Is your garage really a closet? If it contains five or more of the following items, answer Yes.
   (a) A bakelite radio from 1937 (b) A shortwave radio (c) A transistor radio (d) Any other type of radio (e) A quart jar filled with rubber bands (f) A cardboard box full of eight-track tapes (g) A stack of *Look* magazines (h) Broken, rusting tools on a disintegrating pegboard (i) Any musical instrument (j) Seventeen storm windows that don't fit any frame in the house (k) A cyclotron (l) A plasma separator (m) Four popcorn poppers (n) Hundreds of coffee cans full of buttons, dry pens, and rusty nails (o) A mattress with mysterious pink stains (p) Tires (q) Three incomplete moldy sets of encyclopedias (r) An astrolabe (s) PET computers (t) Rabbit ears (u) A perpetual motion device (v) Small surface-to-air missile (w) A satellite dish (x) A linear accelerator (y) A pith helmet
2. Do you believe that physical intimacy between consenting adults can only be achieved with special tools? If Yes, do these tools include three or more of the following?
   (a) Eight-track tapes (b) Latex (c) Zippers (d) Snaps (e) Mirrors (f) A

flat, grainy surface that generates friction (g) Socks (h) Industrial-strength lubricants (i) Ten-foot poles (j) Ball bearings (k) Black lights (l) A thesaurus or dictionary (m) A pith helmet (n) A wet suit (o) Legal forms releasing one of liability (p) Swathes of bandages (q) Fingernail polish (r) Flimsy underthings (s) A large gyroscope

CHAPTER 7

THE FUTURE

PEACE OF MIND, FROM THE SCIENTIFIC PERSPECTIVE

Many Scientists are perpetually disturbed. The constant struggle to verify data produces the most excruciating pain. This helps to explain why Scientists often seem irritable. But only partly. That ignorance is a nagging thorn in the side of many in the Scientific community cannot be disputed, but there is something else afoot here.

Many of the ruddy lads and lasses who first choose the route of reproducible experimental proof are trying to prove to themselves that there is order in a universe they have directly experienced as chaotic. Accumulating advanced degrees does little to heal the hurts this quest engenders. At the end of their great journey through Academia, they find to their dismay that they might have tenure and a mortgage on a home thousands of miles from where they grew up, but at the journey's end they have brought their hated selves along on the trip.

This would be of lesser import if an unhappy Scientist were only

a threat to himself. But the whole world waits in terrified expectation for overstrung Scientists to snap.

And snap they do. Usually a Lab Coat Freak-out (LCF) is kept out of the newspapers, as part of a gentlemen's agreement among industry, government, and the media. But what we don't find out from Dan Rather (himself a victim of BSF, or Business Suit Freak-out) may still kill us.

What can you, the lay community, do to help these disquieted researchers?

You could try to empathize, without going so far as to enable. The next time a Scientist becomes irrational in your midst, you could simply leave the room instead of punching him. A modified version of the Heimlich maneuver often serves to render hysterical researchers briefly unconscious. When they come to, they may have forgotten the source of their rage and passion.

Remember that peace of mind is not distributed evenly. For every blissed-out humanist, there's a tortured Scientist at the helm of some pretty sophisticated (and potentially lethal) machinery.

But there is a simple solution. You could replace that tortured Scientist at the helm with yourself. You could be a free Scientist, a clear Scientist, a Scientist with all Bobs of the spirit holding their hands aloft, like Bill and Al and Tipper and Hillary in the campaign arena of the soul.

In this penultimate chapter, I'll show you how.

THE MOMENT OF CLARITY

We trudge through existence waiting for something to change. We don't know what that something is, and we don't know how we want it to change, but we only know we're waiting.

By the time we realize that we've put our lives on hold waiting for the indefinable to happen, it's too late. We're stuck in our darkened bedrooms, with back problems, a closet full of unworn shoes, and nothing else to show for our lives. No, the time to accept and embrace reality is now.

Change may come, but there's no point in waiting for it. Realization of this fact takes many forms, but in all cases it involves a sudden insight. A hole breaks in the dark clouds. Sunlight streams through. We experience a moment of clarity, which may be brief or protracted.

This Scientist's moment of clarity lasted most of an afternoon. I was a mere stripling at the time. It was a fall day. I was walking in the woods just outside of town, on my way to my local dump to study the effects of oxidation on certain automotive parts.

It was that time of year when a certain melancholy hangs in the air. An almost tangible *tristesse* surrounded me as I lurched through the woods, trying in some vague, intuitive way to find the junkyard. Finally, a pungent odor caught my keen, bladelike nostrils and I followed the olfactory lead.

The scent led me to leave the woods and enter a clearing. There, spread about me in a seemingly never-ending chain of small mounds, was the discarded produce of the city in which I lived. An immense, unexpected, and unfamiliar feeling of gratitude filled me. I lost the strength in my legs and fell to the ground.

With one eye in the mulch and the other wildly surveying the sky, I suddenly knew with absolute certainty that all was well with the universe. That no matter what accidents of fate should befall me in the future, some things, like garbage and clumsiness, would always remain constant.

Unfortunately, one cannot manufacture these moments at will. They arise from chance or celestial manipulation, never at the whim of the observer.

There are, however, certain techniques that make the job of waiting for enlightenment easier. These techniques involve the manipulation of the boredom threshold.

But first we must define boredom. Science defines boredom as the "painful and melancholy situation of having no data to manipulate." Non-Scientists get bored because they don't realize that the lack of data to manipulate is the reason behind their boredom. Faced with the prospect of boredom, the Scientist can turn his energies toward a dramatic and perhaps even dangerous experiment, but the bored non-Scientist will probably just watch television.

But both Scientist and non-Scientist still find themselves between a rock and a hard place. Both employ temporary solutions of dangerous experimentation and television-watching, but boredom, alas, cannot be wished away. Only painful and deep inner healing can dig out the rotten foundation that underlies chronic *ennui*.

There is another solution: to use the techniques outlined below.

These techniques cannot be found anywhere else, and in themselves would justify whatever you paid for this book.

SENSITIVITY AND THE SCIENTIST

Any Scientific instrument must be calibrated in order to be effective. The size of a window of opportunity affects its signal/noise ratio, an important barometer of cost-effectiveness. Human sensitivity can be quantified and measured, despite the protestations of secular humanists and would-be poets.

For example, when romantic poet William Wordsworth declared, "The World is too much with us, late and soon!" he was anticipating "Purple Rain," rocker Prince's paean to the English lake country. On a scale measuring sensitivity and number of volumes in print, both lyricists could be assigned an equivalent rating (even though to some degree we would be comparing apples with oranges).

Wordsworth and Prince earned the undying devotion of millions of fans, but their sensitivity came at great personal cost. All true sensitives are profoundly unhappy. They have long delicate fingers, aquiline nostrils that flare in moments of passion, wrists and temples covered with translucent skin that shows a skein of delicate blue veins just beneath the surface, and a tendency to swoon in high-pressure situations. It's no picnic.

So a Scientist's first technique is *insensitivity*. Fortunately, few Scientists are in the least bit sensitive. Those choosing to dabble in the creative arts are just trying to impress potential sex partners. Oh, occasionally a Scientist will attend a poetry reading held in the employee cafeteria, but only to make a favorable impression on that special someone.

If a Scientist ever attempts to read his or her poetry, go to the nearest phone and dial 911. Many states reward whistle-blowers.

PRODUCTIVITY

Most things that are fun to do are destructive to property, self-esteem, and general health. Though this is no one's fault, we can moderate our behavior to minimize the damage.

Instead of having a whole lot of fun, just horse around a bit. As a result, life may be Colorized rather than Technicolor, and the soundtrack may lack the thundering bass and searing highs of Sensurround, but there won't be a Piper to pay when the credits roll.

In fact, this new Least Common Denominator Life will be all the rage at the beginning of the next century. As the standard of living falls, we'll lower our expectations and adjust our behavior accordingly.

Even home entertainment will adopt a mutated information-delivery system that adjusts for postliterate tolerance levels. Instead of twenty-four hours a day television will operate a mere twenty-four minutes a day. A quick scan with my Time Machine (The Eon Blaster 3000™ Version 5.2) reveals the following programs on your home screen, in their entirety, on the Attention Span Channel:

How're Yer Vowels?

Contestant Number One	Is it an "e"? (Buzzer sounds.)
Emcee	No, I'm sorry, it's not an "e."
Contestant Number Two	Is it an "a"? (Fire alarm; buzzer; fanfare.)
Emcee	"A" is right! The Hawaiian cruise is yours! (The end.)

Honey, the Kids Are Toast!

Harried Mother	No, you can't.
Whining Teenager	Aw Mom, please?
Harried Mother	Oh, all right. (Laughter of recognition; prolonged applause.) (The end.)

Lethal Buddy, Fatal Weapon!

Cop	I'm taking you off the street!

Drug Dealer	Try it, cop! (Gunshot.)
Drug Dealer	Ow!
Cop	Book him. (The end.)

By the end of the twenty-first century, according to my projections, our collective idea of a good time will be just sitting, staring at the wallpaper, which will produce an interior design comeback around 2073.

THE POWER OF NEGATIVE THINKING

As any newsperson can tell you, negativity sells. Sure, people like a cute puppy rescue story every once in a while, but mainly they're interested in dirt. Well, the future can make your life much more saleable if you turn even the smallest of your problems into a sensational catastrophe!

If you can never hope to have a made-for-TV movie based on your problems, you could still enjoy local notoriety by airing your dirty laundry in as conspicuous a way as possible.

Be creative. The next time someone asks you, "How are you?" reply, "Pretty well, considering. . . ." Then make a long face and sigh. If that doesn't prompt an inquiry into the details of your life, the other party doesn't know you from chopped liver anyway.

The real power in negativity, though, comes from projecting it onto others. Always assume the worst of others. Suspect that your spouse is cheating on you or hoarding your joint resources in a secret savings account. Convince yourself that your business associates gossip about you behind your back. Make the worst-case scenario your game plan, and don't deviate from it. Keep an "oops" near your lips, and let your most frequent ejaculation be "Well, what did you expect anyway?" Let negativity gallop unbridled around your brain! If you keep your expectations low, they will always be filled, and often exceeded. Genuinely good things will happen without the least bit of prodding from you. Then you can take a tip from politicians and take credit for these synchronistic surprises. Yes, for the real opportunist, every day is Christmas!

LEARNING TO BLAME EFFECTIVELY

Effective blame is an acquired and delicate skill. After all, pointing the finger at others only encourages others to point theirs at you. If like most of us you've been less than scrupulous in your affairs, retro-blame can be troublesome. But experience and training can help you avoid it. All Scientists must become expert at blaming, at passing the buck. In fact, doing this convincingly is the very essence of Science.

Blaming is a Scientifically creative act, which allows you to feel temporary feelings of superiority, the same feelings an artist has at the moment of inspiration! As your blaming skills grow, these feelings will evolve in both duration and intensity. This growth and the emotional rewards that come with it depend on a carefully constructed foundation.

Where, how, and why have the ones you blame done their shameful deeds? Are they still concealing their acts? How will they justify their actions? What would you do if you were in their shoes?

Let's get specific. Say your lab partner has forgotten to put away the glassware at the end of the workday. You want to hurt your lab partner at least as badly as he has hurt you.

Merely reminding him will only cause him to grumble a lame apology and clean up after himself. But as time goes on, nothing will have really changed and you will still feel cheated, abused, and resentful.

You could, of course, "own" these feelings, but since it's really all your lab partner's fault, why should you?

Now let's imagine a scenario using Active Blaming(TM). Constantly refer to your lab partner only as "Piggy." Whenever the occasion presents itself, simply say, "Well, Piggy, at least when

I'm done working I put my glassware away.'' Then puff out your cheeks like a blowfish, exhale noisily, cluck your tongue, and roll your eyes.

Eventually your lab partner will begin to feel badly, without knowing precisely why. Your subtle, nagging behavior will begin to make an impression. Over time this impression will become a dent in his character, eventually precipitating the behavior you desire.

There's always a chance he may be too insensitive to get the message. If so, you can always take time after work to dip his glassware in pancake syrup.

CREATIVE DAWDLING

You're never not doing something. At the bare minimum your heart is beating and you're breathing. Your mind is active, at some level of consciousness. So give yourself credit for that at least and let yourself off the hook emotionally.

Let your gaze drift over the scene in front of you. If you're propped up in the bathtub, where so many creative dawdlers find themselves, then you're looking at some soapy water with your knees and toes breaking the surface a few feet in front of you. Now, in this position, or curled in the fetal position on your lounger or *longue*, you are probably relaxed enough to try an experiment.

First: Try to imagine doing something that does not involve spending money, ingesting psychotropic substances, or inflicting yourself on someone else sexually.

Hard to do, isn't it? Drawing a blank, aren't you? That's okay. It's to be expected. After all, you've spent most of your life doing the same things over and over again. Let's try something a little easier.

Take a look at your life so far.

Remember, one definition of insanity is the insistence that your life is the screenplay to a major motion picture that hasn't been made yet. Some believe that the only reason the movie hasn't been made is that casting the lead roles has proven too difficult. Others believe that the picture has been made and is doing fantastic business in foreign markets.

It takes humility and great self-honesty to admit there is no movie. Never has been, never will be. This is it. Nobody's watching but me. To admit this may be the hardest thing any of us ever do.

So don't be insane. Look back honestly on what you've done and what you've failed to do. Everything comes out in the wash, even the worst stains. Time is a great laundry, and often the change machine is broken. We search and search, but there is no attendant. There is nothing to do but scrawl a pathetic demand for someone to fix this place up. We go home and curse Fate, the Laundromat, and our Lives in general.

Wouldn't it be better if we piled the dirty clothes into the back of the car and drove, thousands of miles if need be, until we found a cool mountain stream and some rocks, then stopped and banged out the dirt in the pristine environs of nature as our forebears did? Maybe.

CREATIVE VISUALIZATION

All I know is, true Scientists channel creativity only into those areas that reward experimentation. As a person trying to release the Scientist inside, you are no exception.

You are possessed of a mind that can visualize great things. However, you may be unaware of the power in that mind of yours. Who can blame you for not understanding the gray walnut in your skull? What has it done for you lately? But now Creative Dawdling has changed you. You're ready to challenge your formerly atrophied brain. You can begin to visualize something better. Let's try some alternative scenarios for you and see if anything rings a bell.

SCENARIO #1

You are the president of a multinational corporation. Tens of thousands of employees work under you. The major job of this corporation is to denude the rain forests of the Amazon. So far you have made excellent progress.

One day when you report to work you notice protesters holding picket signs. They are blocking the main entrance to the building your corporation owns. Instead of challenging them, you give them a speech. You tell them you were once an idealist too. Once you drove a battered twelve-year-old Volkswagen and bought most of your clothes secondhand.

Then you grew up and decided to go after power and wealth. And now you have achieved your goals and are happier than you've ever been. Happier than any of the protesters could ever be.

The police arrive and begin herding the protesters into paddy wagons. You see several protesters glaring at you as they are led away, but you detect envy in their malice. You go to work feeling you've accomplished something, even though it's only 9:00 A.M.

SCENARIO #2

You are a concert violinist. The instrument you play is a Stradivarius, worth more than the gross national product of many Third World countries.

You spend most of the year on the road, performing in identical large auditoriums on college campuses. Most of the time you have no idea where you are, but you manage to do the job on autopilot. Sometimes you think you're going to snap and do something outrageous, like pull down your pants while performing. You contemplate getting professional help, but then things seem better the next day so you just move on to another college town.

Just when you think you might do something scandalous, it

occurs to you that you don't really enjoy being a concert violinist. You'd rather repair VCRs or shoes. So one bright spring morning in Indiana you simply drop out of sight. You change your name and enroll in a trade school. Eventually you forget all about the violin and settle in a trailer court on the edge of town.

All right, let's examine these two visualizations. Which one would benefit the Scientist? Which one the non-Scientist? In fact, does Science have anything to do with creative visualization?

Of course it does, otherwise it wouldn't be a chapter in this book. But what exactly is the Science of Creative Visualization?

Let's answer that question with another question. If you could be an animal, which animal would you be?

If you're a Gemini with a Taurus rising, chances are you'd choose to be an anteater. We ought to know, because those are our astrological signs, and we have often admired the anteater.

Long of snout and covered with a shaggy coat, the anteater has a job few envy. Yet his opportunities are as numerous as ants. Likewise, few choose to be Scientists, but the opportunities for advancement are as numerous as the atoms that make up so-called reality.

HOPE FOR THE FUTURE

There is no hope for the future. There can't be, because hope only exists in the present. And yet we all must confess a certain fondness for the idea that tomorrow may dawn on a world that is somehow less jaded, less flatulent, less self-pitying, less mean-spirited.

Of course, such hopes are foolish. The facts simply do not justify them. But who could call himself a Scientist who did not, at least occasionally, fudge the facts?

Speaking of fudge, did you know that an almost edible fudge-like substance can be found at the bottom of any operating nuclear reactor? It must drip from the control rods or something. Perhaps it's a mutated form of graphite. That's what it tastes like anyway, something like sucking on pencil lead.

But I digress. We were talking about the future.

In the future I will lose weight. I will regain the youthful optimism that once prompted me to stay up every night for a week trying to debug a computer program that evaluated the statistical probability for severe dandruff in sheep. I will find a new bounce in my step. I will burst into song for no apparent reason. (Once, in 1959, after ingesting a mild sedative and listening to an early John Coltrane album, I sang Doris Day's ''Que Sera Sera'' for thirty-six consecutive hours.)

When we finally arrive at the end of the road, will we be welcomed by a gray-haired granny and offered a soothing cup of herbal tea, or will we be beaten by a gang of insolent teenagers? The answer lies in what we do with our time today.

This Scientist rests assured that he is building for himself a magnificent edifice of stone and steel, a burnished sarcophagus that will bear mute witness that there was once a laboratory where things got done right the first time, where tax dollars spent equaled progress with a capital *P*, where work-study students—enthusiastic, wholesome, grateful!—cleaned the glassware until it was spotless, until it shone in the sun that streamed in through dustless Venetian blinds.

GUFF

Never take any guff from anybody. Don't associate with strangers bearing guff. The truth is, you have no way of knowing where that guff has been. You can purchase pharmaceutical-quality guff, of course, but only with a special permit obtainable directly from the FDA. They only give out two a year (last year it was to two postal inspectors doing legitimate research into circulatory problems among sheep). Again, leave guff to those constitutionally empowered to handle it. 'Nuff said.

FYI...

Now that you're a true Scientist, you should know this already, but does a stitch in time save nine?

Yes. As long as a base-ten numeral system is used. Binary stitches save a whopping 10100110, but those stitches are the new digital stitches. They have wonderful specifications but are annoying to look at and even more annoying to wear. Then there's the type of stitch called the null-set stitch, favored by nudists, who go out without a stitch on. From this Scientists theorize that they sometimes go out without a stitch off. In this case, the double negative would self-cancel and they would be fully dressed. So even a stitch in time must obey the laws of mathematics and logic in order to equal nine.

On the other hand, if you were to take 10 milliliters of a 3 Normal solution of potassium hydroxide and add it to 5 milligrams of a mildly radioctive halide (bromine 57 or iodine 63), it may affect the well-being of someone besides yourself.

The key word here is *may.* It depends on your motives. Are you just horsing around or do you have some higher purpose in mind? Anyone can end life as we know it, but it takes a scholar to tear down and build up simultaneously. We Scientists are in the business of juggling priorities as well as molecules. We must dare to admit to ourselves our true motives for doing that on which we dare to spend hefty grant dollars. That's why whenever I play with radioactive substances or blow up something, I take a Rorschach test first, just to be safe.

TO DO AND SEE

It's time for a full confession. Only after a thorough housecleaning will we be able to look the Supreme Scientist in the eyes and say, "Experiment completed, Sir!"

Fudging the data to fit your expectations, or manipulating the rigors of the Scientific method to protect or coddle a lab partner, results only in heartbreak.

Trouble is, many in the Scientific community have forgotten what it feels like to tell the truth. They couldn't do it even if they wanted to. So we have taken the liberty of composing a Scientist's Confession, with blank spaces for the details of your specific transgressions:

> I admit now, for the first time ever, that I have not been telling the whole truth. In fact, often I have not told anything even close to the truth. My examination of ______ was colored by my interest in proving that ______ is the main reason behind ______, and when the experimental data failed to point in that direction, I changed it.
>
> Once I started on this path, it became alarmingly easy to continue and even expand upon my deceptions. Since they were all my deceptions, they agreed with each other, and this made it even easier to continue. Remember the research that brought me fame and honor—the ______? Well, not only was the research itself falsified, I didn't even do most of it. The majority was done by graduate students and undergraduates on work/study; the rest was simply copied out of obscure Eastern European journals.
>
> Most of the grant money I received from ______ was spent on an extended vacation in ______, where I wrestled with my conscience and an ever-increasing addiction to ______. I think that I have it under control now, or at least it's better than it was.
>
> So I'm sorry. I know I've lied, and I've compromised not only my work but the work of hundreds in related fields. I can't pay back the money. I don't have it anymore. I suppose this means the end of my career. I guess I'll be lucky to find a job teaching Science at a junior high school.

Feels good, doesn't it? Even the ugly truth isn't as ugly as our worst fears. You'll find that your posture will improve from now on. You'll stand up straighter, shoulders back, chin up. It's like being Rolfed without the discomfort or the expense.

THE FINAL CHAPTER: YOUR DREAM HOUSE

CONGRATULATIONS, SCIENTIST!

The unachievable dream of the latter half of the twentieth century has been to have it all. Feminism has led women to believe that they can have a career, kids, a loving other, a hobby, daily exercise, and perpetually youthful skin as soft as a calf's nose. Capitalism has led men to believe that they are God's gift to the universe. They can have a dark suit, a power tie, and a secretary/wife/maid; they can have comfort and wealth attach to them like leeches; they can throw their dirty socks in any damn corner they feel like.

But, as this book has shown, happiness, like perfect toast, is impossible. All we can really hope for is a subterranean humanoid-free life-style in which children and other small annoying creatures keep out of our way. To do that, you need a Dream House. Well, lucky you. Thanks to your new Scientific Attitude, all you need to do is visualize and it's yours.

NO NEED TO WIPE YOUR FEET

Chances are the details of your Dream House make a roadmap to your personality. My Dream House is no different from yours in that respect, but it is a different house, because we are by no means the same person. Therefore I can't comment on your Dream House, though I'll bet you don't live in it. I live in mine. The Fortress of Arrogance.

The road to the Fortress of Arrogance, like the road to your Dream House, is full of the same detours, minimum-service access lanes, and narrow bridges that should have been replaced years ago. And yet I like it that way. Likewise, my Dream House is filled with warped particle board, frayed wiring, and cracked linoleum. I know every fray and crack. They exude that invisible odor of comfort. They smell like me. The difference lies not only in our various scents, but in our degrees of enlightenment. After all, I've been a Scientist all my life. You're just embarking on that austere road.

I try to meet with laypeople (non-Scientists) at least once a day as a kind of reality check. Yesterday, for instance, I met with the finance minister of F______, a small island nation off the coast of Borneo. We ended up having a somewhat philosophical discussion about the influence of alchemy on the Bessemer process. Then after lunch I had a lengthy discussion with a pizza delivery person, in which I tried to explain molecular weight in terms he would understand.

Imagine that *you've* come to visit me in my Dream House. No need to knock at the door, there isn't one. Just ring the bell, then wait while I open the airlock. A distinctive whish of air and a section of the wall opens. That's your cue. Come on down!

Step into the module and press LL. Brace yourself and hold on to your stomach as you drop twenty stories at a dizzying eighty miles per hour. As you come gently to a halt, the doors whiff open, just like the doors on the Starship *Enterprise*! As you emerge, pull aside the hanging, mildewed carpet remnant—a souvenir from my very first lab. That orange stain is Iodine 131. It's still mildly radioactive, but probably harmless if you don't linger. Let your eyes adjust to the relative darkness. It isn't actually dark in here, but the soft wash of infrayellow light doesn't seem bright at first. There I am, comfortably ensconced in my sagging davenport. I wear my davenport like a garment. In fact, it's the only garment I am wearing. I strategically shift the pillows to lessen your discomfort. I want you to feel at home here in my Dream House. It is, of course, a clothing-optional environment, just like my lab. As always, I seem to be the only one exercising the clothing-free option. And speaking of exercise, would you like to see my gym?

Look at all the chromium/molybdenum tubing shining under bright halogen lights! If that rowing machine looks vaguely like a centrifuge, it's because it is just that. In fact, many of my exercise machines do double duty, saving potential grant-givers hundreds of thousands and me much needed floorspace. Down the end of the anodized aluminum corridor, you can see the bank of coffee urns—ready to spew out breakfast or a muscle-relaxing whirpool bath at the push of a button. On your left are the Slumber Tubes, for the convenience of my overnight guests, if I should ever have any.

But wait—that siren suddenly shrieking from the wall is trying to tell us something. Since the lights are dimming there's a very good chance we're approaching some sort of electricial brownout. Perhaps a complete meltdown! You've come at an auspicious time.

I'd like to visit with you more, but there are some things I should attend to. But thank you for stopping by. And as they say down around the Superconducting Supercollider, "Y'all come back now, hear?"

YOUR QUESTIONS

"WHERE IS YOUR DREAM HOUSE?"

Have you ever heard of the White Mountains in Nevada? Deep beneath the crust of the earth's mantle, there's a laboratory containing the world's most sophisticated equipment. Personal and national security considerations prohibit me from saying exactly who lives in that lab, but I'll tell you one thing.

I do not live in Terre Haute, Indiana.

"WHAT ARE HOLIDAYS LIKE AT THE FORTRESS OF ARROGANCE?"

My assistant and I observe the holidays in a rather subdued fashion. First we whip up a few liters of my famous Christmas punch, the recipe for which I'm only to happy to share with you.

Take ninety-nine parts ethanol and one part red food coloring, shirr in a centrifuge, and irradiate with a short-lived halogen isotope—I prefer Iodine 49. After relaxing with a flask or two of this, Rodney and I usually let loose what we really think of each other. Then we trade gifts, and sometimes punches, culminating in a tearful and maudlin make-up session in which we vow not to make the same mistakes next year. Of course, every year we forget and repeat the process. So that's our holiday routine! Thanks for asking!

"SINCE CLOUDS CONTAIN MILLIONS OF GALLONS OF WATER, AND SINCE THE TEMPERATURE UP HIGH IS VERY COLD, THEN CLOUDS HAVE THE POTENTIAL TO FREEZE SOLID AND DROP TO THE EARTH LIKE GLACIERS. HOW DOES THE FORTRESS OF ARROGANCE PROTECT ITSELF FROM ICE MOUNTAINS FALLING IN CHUNKS FROM THE ATMOSPHERE?"

Clouds do fall. How else to explain the flat expanse of Nebraska? Indeed, the whole Midwest was once squished by a fallen thunderhead of gigantic proportions. Thanks to global warming, these events are far less likely today than in our prehistoric past, but cumulonimbus-sicles are still worthy of respect. Every morning before I enter the sarcophagal gloom of the Fortress of Arrogance, my hidden laboratory, I crouch in my tiny Sky Bubble Observatory, scanning the heavens with a pair of 7X50 Bausch & Lombs, looking for aerial frozen death. My rugged ABS roofing offers a degree of security, but if the sky ever does fall, there is no safe place.

"HOW DO I DEAL WITH MY ENVY OF YOUR DREAM HOUSE?"

Imagine that you're me and I'm you. I wake up one morning and realize that instead of living in a wonderful underground laboratory, I'm just a chump with a lousy job, too many kids, and a mate who doesn't understand me. You, on the other hand, are really excited about experimenting with all this cool equipment. You wonder aloud, "How do I turn on the cyclotron?"

You don't. Nobody touches that equipment, especially not me if, God forbid, a form such as yourself were suddenly to occupy my body. That equipment contains a state-of-the-art, top-secret, fully automated death ray that could end all life as we know it should it fall into the wrong hands. No, I cannot entertain your premise, not even hypothetically, because the consequences would be too awful. Stop now, before it's too late. Turn yourself in. Lie down and put your hands out in front of you. The police will be gentle with you, I'll see to that.

A SURVEILLANCE-CAMERA MOMENT AT THE FORTRESS OF ARROGANCE

Dr. Science is standing in the dust-free Science Room, one hand on his powerful Kray, the other carefully pouring an unknown substance from a beaker into a subterranean vat.

Dr. Science	Oops. (Rodney, Dr. Science's trusted assistant, looks up from his clipboard and sniffs the air suspiciously.)
Rodney	What's that smell, Dr. Science?
Dr. Science	Never mind. Keep logging those integers. (Dr. Science removes an unwieldy piece of clothing from the handy walk-in stainless steel closet.)
Rodney	Is that an asbestos suit, Dr. Science?
Dr. Science	(Laughing heartily) Of course not, Rodney. It's spun lead. Here, sign this. (Dr. Science produces a standard release form, as an eerie pale green mist begins to swirl around their feet. Beads of sweat appear on Dr. Science's brow.)
Rodney	(Signing) Is it getting hot in here or is it just me?
Dr. Science	There you go, now this copy—

Rodney	What is this?
Dr. Science	Just a simple form releasing me from all responsibility.
Rodney	Oh, okay.
	(With almost superhuman strength, Dr. Science picks up a large cardboard box from the closet, removes identical forms from it, and thrusts them into Rodney's arms. The pale green mist is at waist level now, and growing thicker.)
Dr. Science	Now take these Rodney, and get them signed. Quickly.
Rodney	(Mutters under breath, heads for door) Where?
Dr. Science	Oh, everybody within, let's see, a fifty-mile radius.
Rodney	(Whining) That'll take days!
Dr. Science	(Sternly) You've got five hours.

Dr. Science snaps his personally designed headgear into place. The green mist grows thicker, forming a fluorescent cloud around his head. A look of pride forms on his features, as Rodney enters the module on his way to perform his nearly hopeless task. Then the scene disappears in a lime green haze.

TO DO AND SEE

A SELF-ACTUALIZATION ESTIMATOR

The following are sample situations that you can react to in any number of ways. How you react to them reflects upon the level of self-actualization you have achieved.

SITUATION #1

A man knocks on your door. He is seven feet tall and is very well dressed. When you open the door he doesn't say anything for a while. Shifting his weight from foot to foot he looks sadly down at you, as if apologizing for his great height. When he does speak, he mumbles and drools.

You think about closing the door on him, but something about his sad stare and indecipherable speech makes you invite him in. Once in your house he lies down on your living room rug and begins to weep loudly. Even though you are alone in your house, you are very embarrassed.

It becomes apparent that the man is not going to get up. You're going to have to take action.

At this point you: (a) Call the police. (b) Take off your clothes, drop to all fours, and bark like a dog. (c) Light the house on fire. (d) Do nothing and hope the strange man calms down.

SITUATION #2

You're at work trying to finish a project that needs to get done today. It's fifteen minutes until quitting time. A particularly long-winded employee drops by and attempts to tell you all about her latest vacation.

You pretend to listen but keep on with your work. She drones on, and you mutter short exclamations to make it seem as if you're following her story. Suddenly you realize that she has stopped talking. You look up from your work. She is looking at you expectantly.

It occurs to you that she has asked you a question and is waiting for your reply. At this point you: (a) Admit you haven't been listening and ask her to repeat the question. (b) Say, "Yeah, sure." (c) Call the police. (d) Punch her as hard as you can.

SITUATION #3

You have just entered the massage room at your health club. You disrobe, lie down on the massage table, and cover yourself with a sheet. As you await the arrival of your masseur you notice an odd aroma in the air. Something that smells like creosote, the stuff they put on railroad ties and telephone poles.

When the masseur arrives he is someone you have never seen before. He is wearing dirty overalls and carrying a large sledgehammer, which he drops noisily in the corner. He then picks up a large bucket and holds it over you. From the vapors that come from the bucket, you deduce that it contains boiling creosote. At this moment you: (a) Leap from the massage table and run out of the room. (b) Scream, "Heinrich, Heinrich, the house is on fire!" (c) Call the police. (d) Smile, curl up in a fetal position, and patiently await whatever fate has in store for you.

APPENDIX

ACCOUNTABILITY

We expect and demand accountability from politicians, investment brokers, and teenagers, but few would place this burden on the Scientific community. It would limit their productivity.

If we had the guts to pay our Scientists on a discovery-per-dollar basis, we might get better value for our money. Once that ratio has been fixed, we could really chart Scientific progress. The morning newspaper would be full of colorful bar graphs comparing our Scientists to theirs, charting the advance or decline of American Science. And once Scientists achieve a quantified productivity, they could be traded like baseball players. Scientists would save their best work for sweeps periods, when the ratings were determined.

All this would ensure a new link between Science and public relations. NASA has already had one publicist, the former vice president, but other wings of the Scientific establishment will no doubt be more selective in their hiring.

ANN B. DAVIS

This popular character actress is an anomaly. She seems immune to aging. She has been fifty now for almost forty years. Like Walter Brennan, who seemed to be age sixty throughout his career, and Dick Clark, who still looks thirty-five, she may

have unique physical properties that react to the so-called Hollywood rays that emanate from motion picture cameras and sometimes serve to affect the aging process.

Unlike some stars, like Michael Jackson, Cher, and Phyllis Diller, who use artificial means to keep themselves youthful, Ann B. Davis seems to have remained fifty entirely naturally. She certainly warrants further study.

THE BIG HEAT

As a postwar whodunit this Glenn Ford starrer is exciting enough, but is of interest to Science only in its depiction of coffee being put to highly inappropriate uses.

THE BRADY BUNCH

Details about this popular television series remain sketchy, but I think we can safely assume the following:

The Brady Bunch, studies reveal, is the story of a lovely lady who was bringing up three very lovely girls. All of them had hair of gold like their mother (the youngest one in curls). It's also the story of a man named Brady, who was busy with three boys of his own. They were four men living all together. Yet, ironically, they were all alone.

One day, according to my research, the lady met this fellow and they knew it was much more than a hunch (it may have been an hypothesis of some kind, we don't know) that this group should somehow form a family. To the best of our knowledge, that's how they became the Brady bunch. Those of you familiar with the program are of course free to question my data.

HOUSEHOLD GODS

Cast of *Beverly Hills, 90210*
Easter Bunny
Elvis
Fergie
Madonna
The McLaughlin Group
Oprah
Princess Di
Ross Perot
Santa Claus
Tooth Fairy
Bart Simpson

LEVELS OF HELL

Besides the levels mentioned in the text, some characteristic levels in the 6,543 circles of hell include:

- You're on a campaign bus for eternity, singing the title songs from Elvis movies with Al, Bill, Hillary, and Tipper.
- You're trapped in a shopping mall with George Bush, forever.
- You are a Honda dealer in Detroit, until the end of time.
- Not knowing the language, you must go to France and make them reconsider Jerry Lewis and Mickey Rourke.
- You must teach the classics, in the original Latin and Greek, in a suburban junior high school.

MOVIES AVAILABLE ON LIQUID CRYSTAL DISPLAY

There are two.

Nev Donau Vistetlii is an unsubtitled foreign film (from an Eastern European country which must remain nameless for fear of reprisals). I have seen this movie countless times, and can still make no sense of it. It stars two bearded men in overcoats and appears to have something to do with a missing potato. There's also a stocky woman in a leotard who appears from time to time, but her function in the film appears to be mainly symbolic. The film may even be a travelogue of some sort, rather than art—I don't know, and frankly don't care. It is precious to me for its format, nothing else.

The other film is an in-house documentary made for a chronometer trade show, called *Tomorrow's Wristwear Today!*

MY FORMER WIVES

In no particular order they were: Elaine, who disapproved of the hogan; Georgeann, who was always irrationally insisting that I talk to her; Roxie and Muriel, frail creatures, who both had nervous breakdowns; Suzanne, whose attempts at interior design I foiled at every turn; and a rather striking woman with red hair, whose name I have blocked. I simply awoke one morning and she was gone. I don't know what her problem was.

NIILSOEN EXIT POLL

(Translated from the ancient Erse by Dr. Science)

You have fought well and bravely. Now as thy heads on special posts are put, prepare thy warrior spirits to enter the Vestibule of the Valiant! Before you go, would you mind answering a few questions?

1. How did you first hear that our fierce invaders were flying hither? (a) Group vision in menstrual hut (b) Premonition by village sage
2. If (b), where were the signs read of our coming? (a) Goat entrails (b) Stars (c) Spoor of wild beasts (d) Runes
3. Any different tribes, if choice you had, would you rather have put your crops and building to the torch? (a) Berserkers from the frozen north (b) Wiry horsemen from the Orient (c) Rigid Roman centuries marching in formation (d) Jutes
4. Be you satisfied with the thoroughness of our sacking? Aye/Nay.

5. State religious preference. "I worship: (a) earth." (b) sky." (c) Green Man." (d) Womanspirit." (e) rocks." (f) bad weather."
6. State sex. If (M) art thou (a) farmer? (b) hunter/gatherer? (c) warrior? (d) seer?
   If (W) art thou (a) farmer? (b) breeder? (c) warrior goddess? (d) seer?
7. If you are Woman and Niilsoen spares thee, state life-style preference. (a) Breeder (b) Common chattel (c) Concubine for Fjorn the Vehement
8. Are thou (a) 1–10 (b) 10–15 (c) 15–20 (d) 20–25 (e) 25–30 years of age?

Thank you for your cooperation. Die bravely!

OKLAHOMA AUGURIES

Here follows the mysterious text channeled by Dr. Science in a hotel room one fateful afternoon in Oklahoma, in its entirety:

Bob/Bob
Two Bobs
Swinger/swingsets
Dad/Cool Cat Daddy
Supermodel/supermom
Work/sleep
Up/down
In/out
Synchronicities!
Contradictions!
Ann B. Davis/Ann B. Davis
Pick up shirts/pay gas bill
Ow/buy aspirin
New methodology for data assimilation?

OZONE

Ozone is basically hypertriplicated oxygen, with carbon monoxide thrown in for flavor. It is created whenever the fourth dimension, or space/time continuum, rips. Until the rip heals, ozone escapes, in much the same way that the aromatic smell of rich coffee wafts from a bag of whole coffee beans when you stomp on it. After a thunderstorm, that clean fresh scent we smell is ozone. When we visit Los Angeles, the sharp burning smell that greets us when we step off the plane is also ozone! Ozone is the ultimate Buddhist substance, everything and nothing, both at the same time.

THE REAL REALTOR?

If this book has taken a harsh look at Realtors, it is only because its author believes that Realty, like Science, is a calling, a vocation. Unfortunately, most who answer that call just don't have what it takes.

Deep down, you see, we are all potential Realtors. Most of us have not taken the opportunity to develop that facet of our personalities, and for good reason. To be a real Realtor, one must be willing to be absolutely real. Really real.* We must be ready to stop hiding behind anyone or anything.

Since most of us embrace our many masks as the only real substance of our personality, we are understandably reticent to stand buck naked in the cold winds of truth.

Fortunately, there is One who came before us who can show us the way. He/She is the Universal Realtor, and this entity can be summoned at will, if you know the proper ritual, are pure at heart, and meet certain minimum financial requirements.

First, take all the canceled checks you can find and pile them around you in a circle. Some of us may have a pile many feet high, some a feeble puddle on the floor. It doesn't matter how big the pile, but it is important that you have all of them.

Next lay your credit cards out in a line, directly in front of you. Include department store cards, gas cards, as well as the familiar bank cards. Take off all your clothes and begin to roll in a circle, being careful to roll over all the checks. As you're rolling repeat the following phrase, "Life is meaningless, art is a phantom, only property endures."

Now, stand and strike yourself sharply with your credit cards, jabbing them into the spaces between your ribs. Do this hard enough to leave a red mark, but not hard enough to break the skin.

You'll find yourself crying out in pain and surprise, and you will gradually notice the presence of another emotion—gratitude. The tears that form in your eyes will eventually be grateful tears, tears of joy. Joy that you even have a checkbook, charge cards, and that you can stop this jabbing process whenever you like.

Soon you will fall, delirious, to the floor. Sleep will overtake you. When you awaken, you'll be cold, somewhat confused, but life will taste different. Your relationship with money will have changed. And more important, you will be one step closer to being real. Really real.

THE SEVEN WONDERS OF THE WORLD

SILICON VALLEY

Contrary to current belief, Silicon Valley did not become the center of the computer industry because of its massive silicon deposits. No, its success was largely due to the huge LCD lake just north of San Jose, even though this lake is invisible when

**Really Real* is a registered trademark of Self Actualized Realtors, Inc.

viewed from most oblique angles. Blind trout swim in that lake, I'm told. I'm also told they're quite tasty when poached. I wouldn't know. I don't eat the flesh of blind animals.

BIOSPHERE

This visionary project in the Sunbelt has attracted a lot of heat from so-called investigative journalists. Every time fit, good-looking people don attractive orange uniforms and enter a hermetically sealed environment that duplicates in miniature the various climates of the earth, there's always some cynical unshaven reporter yelling ''Foul!'' So what if they charge admission for tourists to sneak peeks at them? So what if they snuck out a couple times for sandwiches? Does this make the biosphere bad Science? If the biosphere is bad Science, then the Fortress of Arrogance is bad Science. This is impossible. The simple truth is there's no such thing as bad Science. There are only data and lack of data. Better fudged facts than no facts at all.

EURODISNEY

That any French are attending this theme park at all is proof that anything is possible.

THE FORTRESS OF ARROGANCE

TIME MACHINE

The Eon Blaster 3000™ Version 5.2. I invented it (or *will* invent it, to be accurate) in the year 2011, and went back in time (or will go back) to 1956, where I presented it to myself as a wedding present on the occasion of my third marriage, to Roxie. Unfortunately, my future self chose to hang around the reception, and drink rather more than he was accustomed to. Knowing how the marriage turned out, he began regaling Roxie with stories of my relationships in the future, causing the poor woman to collapse in terror. The marriage was annulled, but of course I knew it would be. Such are the wonders and terrors of time travel.

THE SHOPPING MALL

THE SPHINX

SURPRISE

This is something of a non sequitur, but certain rumors have been flying and I thought I'd take this opportunity to nip them in the bud.

For the record then, I recall meeting George Bush only once, in Paris. I think it was the fall of 1980, October, if I remember correctly. Mr. Bush was running for vice president then, I believe. We were having dinner with some Iranian businessmen. I can't remember what we discussed at dinner exactly. I was there to give George some technical advice on radioactive decay rates, or some related topic. I'm not sure he even knew who I was. Every time I tried to get his attention, he would propose a toast to the eternal friendship between our two countries. He would laugh, the Iranians would frown, and I would mumble something about the half-life of plutonium. I had the veal scallopini, which was very good. Of course it should have been, at those prices.

THE TWELVE REASONS TO LIVE

1. Live, to see what happens in China after communism fails.
2. To see what happens in Cuba when Fidel Castro passes on.
3. How will Murphy Brown's kid turn out?
4. Will Dan Quayle find the dignity he craves?
5. Suicide would mean missing subsequent sequels to *Lethal Weapon*.
6. Your enemies would gloat.
7. You would miss the latest trends in popular music.
8. You would never learn to divide by zero.
9. Elvis is still alive, isn't he? Do you think you're better than Elvis?
10. Someone, sometime, will develop the all-purpose, one-size-fits-all allen wrench that will change the face of technology as we know it. Why can't that someone be you?
11. Who would feed the fish?
12. We're all going to be crushed by a giant asteroid anyway.

THE TWO BOBS THEORY

"For every Bob, there is an equal and opposite Bob." Once we reconcile these two forces in our life, we achieve an equilibrium, allowing us to become one with the universe, and join the entropic process, already in progress.

GLOSSARY

Accumulate: Common question asked of tardy persons.
Ambient: Vehicle used to take injured persons to a hospital.
Anteater: Unpopular pet.
Autonomic: Outmoded type of transmission.
Baking Soda: Baking powder with an attitude.
Bathroom: Seat of dysfunction.
Bioengineering: Accessory used by female cyborg to set off her hairstyle.
Cathay: Popular girls' name.
Cats: A musical.
Celtic: Member of a basketball team.
Centrifuge: Blender issued to qualified Scientists.
Chakra: Popular disco singer from the seventies.
Children: The hideous burden of evolution.
Chore: Certainly; you bet; that's a roger, etc.
Cinnabar: Precious herb.
Cistron: Little thingie that sticks out of cell.
Clone: Amusing painted figure in a circus.
Codependent: Your mother; your father; your lover; your child; your neighbor; your pet; your self; etc.
Coffee: Miracle food.
Cognitive: Overrated sense.
Color Code: System used to file data better thrown away.
Consultant: The world's most useless profession.
Converse: Type of shoe.

Cyclotron: What a true Scientist uses to ride to work.
Data: An amusing cyborg on *Star Trek: The Next Generation*.
Decaf: Beverage from hell.
Dedicated Phone Line: Phone used for song requests on AM radio stations.
Demographic: A cluster of consumer quirks.
Digitize: An ophthalmological disorder found only in accountants.
Disenfranchised: One who has lost the lease on a fast-food chain outlet.
Dubious: The so-called eighth dwarf.
Dysfunctional: Normal.

Elastomeric: Property unique to roofing.
Electricity: Force from hell.
Electron: Outmoded political slogan.
Elvis: Popular musical saint.
Emollient: What Molly becomes after three spins in a linear accelerator.
Endorphins: Rare aquatic mammals.
Eschew: Tiny sneeze.
Ethylene Propylene Diene Monomer: A chemical compound.
Exoskeleton: Former oskeleton.
Facts: Dreams.
Faeries: Obsolete beings.
Fax: Instant gratification.
Fiber Optic: Means by which instant data gratification is accomplished.
Foamcore: The Antichrist of woods.
Gastropod: Unnecessary animal.
Gender: Relative superlative of *gend*, as in "Kinder, gender nation."
Gestalt: The polite response to a tiny sneeze.
Gravity: Enemy to levity.
Guesstimate: Scientific measurement.
Hogan: Protagonist in popular sitcom of the 1960s.
Hologram: The sum of the parts of an ogram.
Home: Mythical place.
Huff: Obsolete vehicle.
Humanoid: Android wannabe.
Hydroponic: Casual greeting among droponics.
Hypertriplicated Oxygen: See **Ozone**.
Iconoclast: Optimist.
Infomercial: Art, in the nineties.
Isobutanol: Miracle substance.
Junk Bond: James' stupid younger brother.
Kudzu: Vine from hell.
Kundalini: Hawaiian god of short waves.
Laser: Opposite of energetic.
Linear: Popular girls' name among baby-boomer parents.
Linear Accelerator: Puberty.
Mall: More than some.
Material: Essential ingredient in the composition of Madonna.
Membrane: What enables mems to think.
Men: Dreadful gender.
Mercurial: Adjective often used to describe the personality of Dr. Science.
Mick Jagger: Wealthy rebel.
Mosaic: The food of life.
Museums: Cultural warehouses.
Narcopheme Ombulators: Another term for sominaptic thrombiles.
Neutrino: Nickname for popular Italian singer from the sixties.
Nomad: Happy.

Noxious: Adjective often used to describe the personality of Dr. Science.
Occupation: Job, employment. (Obsolete.)
Over-the-counter: Handy way to shop.
Oxymoron: An insult frequently thrown at large hooved animals.
Ozone: See **Hypertriplicated Oxygen**.
Paradigm: What we have lost.
Parapets: Twin dogs, for example.
Paramedics: Two surgeons.
Parenthood: Thankless occupation.
Parsec: Unit of stellar distance; also used in Hollywood to measure star power.
Parthenogenic Exulgism: Obsolete biological process.
Penthouse: Tense condo.
Petrie Dish: Birthplace of Dr. Science.
Pharaoh: Former Charlie's Angel.
Pheromes: Plural of Pharaoh.
Phrygian Codes of Mithras: Prehistoric crossword puzzle.
Pith: Rare element used in headgear for jungle explorers and mailpersons; also used to kill frogs.
Planck's Constant: Opposite of "Planck's Fickle."
Plinth: More than one plin.
Poll: A quiz that lets us know what we think about events and personalities over which we have no control.
Polysyllabic: Pre–World War II plastic.
Potash: Residue from a pot fire.
Protean: In favor of adolescence.
Pseudoneuroperous: Extinct flightless bird.
Quality Time: Mythical unit of temporal measurement.
Retarded Hemihydrate Plaster: Popular building material.
Robot: What the world needs now.
Sarcophagus: Where Pharaoh sleeps.
Saw: Adage, saying; always old; *new saws* are called "position papers."
Selenium: Prime ingredient in the chemical composition of Dr. Science.
Sex: Former leisure activity.
Shortwave: Of little interest to professional surfers.
Shrinkage: Shorthand term for our Epoch of Therapy, soon to become the Age of Aquarius.
Slugs: Useless creatures.
Special Interest: What a lobbyist must display when approaching Congress.
Supermodel: See **Pharaoh**.
Symptoms: Popular animated television series.
Television: The Antichrist of communications.
Tetravalent: Enormous tropical fish, popular in Singapore.
Topology: The study of lumps.
Traditional Family Values: Fear, resentment, and belligerence.
Trance Channeling: Cheap vacation.
Turtle: Boring reptile.

UFO: Popular Japanese car.

Ultraviolet: Former protégé of Andy Warhol.

Urban: Wraparound headgear worn by Sikhs.

Venn Diagram: Any time you feel like making one, really. That's the beauty of it.

Virtual Reality: Hallucination in a box.

Voting: Once-popular hobby.

Warehouse: Creature who turns into a storage area whenever the moon is full.

Women: Without this gender, men would still be living in caves.

Wonk: One who swoons at the sight of a flow chart.

Yeast: Where the sun rises.

Zero Tolerance: Phrase used to describe the worldview of Dr. Science.